THE TERROR IN THE FRENCH REVOLUTION

Studies in European History

General Editor: Richard Overy
Editorial Consultants: John Breuilly
　　　　　　　　　　　　Roy Porter

PUBLISHED TITLES

The Terror in the French Revolution

Hugh Gough
Statutory Lecturer in History
University College Dublin

First published in Great Britain 1998 by
MACMILLAN PRESS LTD
Houndmills, Basingstoke, Hampshire RG21 6XS and London
Companies and representatives throughout the world

A catalogue record for this book is available from the British Library.

ISBN 0–333–60139–4

 First published in the United States of America 1998 by
ST. MARTIN'S PRESS, INC.,
Scholarly and Reference Division,
175 Fifth Avenue, New York, N.Y. 10010

ISBN 0–312–17673–2

Library of Congress Cataloging-in-Publication Data
Gough, Hugh.
The terror in the French Revolution / Hugh Gough.
p.   cm.
Includes bibliographical references and index.
ISBN 0–312–17673–2 (pbk.)
1. France—History—Reign of Terror, 1793–1794—Causes.
I. Title.
DC183.5.G64 1998
944.04'4—dc21   97–19539
                                                                    CIP

This book is printed on paper suitable for recycling and made from fully managed and
sustained forest sources.

10   9   8   7   6   5   4   3   2   1
07   06   05   04   03   02   01   00   99   98

Printed in Malaysia

Contents

Note on References

References in the text within square brackets relate to items in the Bibliography, with page numbers in italics, for example [17: *34–5*]

Editor's Preface

The main purpose of this Macmillan series is to make available to teacher and student alike developments in a field of history that has become increasingly specialised with the sheer volume of new research and literature now produced. These studies are designed to present the state of the debate on important themes and episodes in European history since the sixteenth century, presented in a clear and critical way by someone who is closely concerned with the debate in question.

The studies are not intended to be read as extended bibliographical essays, though each will contain a detailed guide to further reading which will lead students and the general reader quickly to key publications. Each book carries its own interpretation and conclusions, while locating the discussion firmly in the centre of the current issues as historians see them. It is intended that the series will introduce students to historical approaches which are in some cases very new and which, in the normal course of things, would take many years to filter down into the textbooks and school histories. I hope it will demonstrate some of the excitement historians, like scientists, feel as they work away in the vanguard of their subject.

The format of the series conforms closely with that of the companion volumes of studies in economic and social history which has already established a major reputation since its inception in 1968. Both series have an important contribution to make in publicising what it is that historians are doing and in making history more open and accessible. It is vital for history to communicate if it is to survive.

R. J. OVERY

1 Historians Disagree: Catastrophe, Circumstance or Cancer?

The French Revolution is the main historical dividing line between the ancien régime and the modern world. It replaced a traditional social order based on hierarchy and privilege with a society founded on the modern principles of individual freedom and equality. Sweeping away the intricate political structures of absolute monarchy perfected in the latter half of the seventeenth century by Louis XIV, it substituted a parliamentary system based on electoral politics and, in doing so, detonated a social and political revolution which combined physical violence with ideological radicalism. Neither France nor the world was ever to be the same again. For although much of the revolution's initial impact was confined to France, it rapidly spilled over into the rest of Europe once the revolutionary wars broke out in 1792. By the time Napoleon sailed over the horizon to his final exile in St Helena after his defeat at Waterloo in 1815, an entire generation of Europeans had felt its influence and a new agenda for world history had been set. Written constitutions, parliamentary government and secular ideology had entered the mainstream of political life. Socialism, nationalism, radicalism and conservatism had emerged as the conflicting ideologies of the future and, perhaps most important of all, the word 'revolution' had changed its meaning and become part of modern political vocabulary [48].

Another new concept to emerge during the revolution was that of political 'terror', a term used not just to describe human fear but a style of government based on it [22]. When the revolution began in 1789 there were high hopes that France would achieve a peaceful transition from an absolutist to a parliamentary monarchy. Yet the extent and pace of change between 1789 and 1791 caused deep political division at home and mounting disquiet abroad. In the spring of 1792 revolutionary politicians tried to resolve their problems by war, but war went badly and terror quickly followed. It had two distinct phases: a 'first terror' of August–September 1792, when the monarchy was overthrown and over 1000 people were slaughtered in prison massacres in Paris; then a second terror between the summer of 1793 and the autumn of 1794, which was marked by government centralisation and systematic political repression. During this later period a Committee of Public Safety monopolised power, the economy was subjected to extensive state control, and the entire population of the country mobilised for the war effort. Up to half a million people were imprisoned for political 'crimes', and revolutionary courts sent more than 16,000 of them to the guillotine [124]. A further 20,000 died in prison before trial, and over 200,000 perished in a brutal civil war in the Vendée in the west of France [145].

Compared with the death toll of twentieth-century wars, these figures seem modest. More people died in the first day of the Battle of the Somme in 1916, or during the civil war in Russia after the 1917 revolution, than were guillotined during the whole of the terror. Stalin's purges in Russia in the 1930s and 1940s, or the Nazi holocaust of the Jews during the Second World War, destroyed far more lives in an infinitely more brutal manner, as did the 'killing fields' of the Khmer Rouge in Cambodia in the mid-1970s. Yet figures alone fail to tell the whole story, for the significance of the French revolutionary terror lies less in its body count than in its purpose and timing. It was carried out not by a traditional tyrant set on consolidating power but by a small minority of politicians who claimed to be acting behalf of the 'people'. For the first – but not the last – time, terror was used in the cause of democracy, and the relevance of the terror of 1793–4 to the more devastating 'democratic' terrors of the twentieth century has prompted historians to ask why it happened and what it achieved. The result has been a split of historical opinion into three broad camps. On the right, conservatives condemn the revolution as a disaster of which terror was an intrinsic part from beginning to end. On the left, socialist historians defend the revolution as an important stage in the growth of liberal democracy and see terror as a tactic used by politicians to defend France and democracy against the threats of counter-revolution and war. Between these two schools, a 'revisionist' group of historians has emerged in recent years who accept that the revolution was an important step in the emergence of modern democracy, but argue that terror was an integral and insidious part of its ideology from the outset. Catastrophe, circumstance or cancer? This is the choice facing the historian of the causes, events, and consequences of the terror.

[i] The view from the right

Right-wing hostility to the revolution goes back to the 1790s, because the events of 1789–94 destroyed feudal society, abolished the monarchy, and undermined the traditional power of the French Catholic Church [180]. During the revolution conservatives tried to explain these events either in terms of a conspiracy or as the result of divine will. A Jesuit priest, the Abbé Barruel, argued that the revolution was the result of a plot, hatched over many centuries by Protestants, Enlightenment thinkers, and Freemasons, with the aim of undermining social and religious stability, and plunging France into chaos. A Swiss commentator, Jacques de Maistre, argued instead that it was divine punishment for human sin, and that a new theocratic world order would later emerge with monarchy and Catholicism triumphant [55]. Both interpretations were the work of eccentric minds clearly bewildered by the cataclysmic events going on around them, but a more balanced and durable explanation had already appeared in 1790 in a book written by the Irish politician Edmund Burke. In his *Reflections on the Revolution in France*, which was quickly translated into several European languages and became one of the fundamental texts of the revolution's critics, Burke argued that the revolution was a catastrophe built on the twin errors of political inexperience and Enlightenment rationalism. Revolutionary politicians, he argued, lacked the political experience needed to carry out fundamental political reform, and were mistakenly applying the abstract logic of rational thought to France's problems at the expense of tradition and experience [21]. For Burke this was a catastrophe, for all social and political change had to be a gradual process, built on experience in a cautious and pragmatic way. The fatal error of the revolution had been to jettison tradition in favour of revolution and experience in favour of reason; the result could only be chaos and terror [39].

Burke's prophetic warnings on the slide that would take place from revolution to terror have been used by conservative historians in their work on the revolution ever since. During the nineteenth century Hippolyte Taine made it a central feature of his *Origins of Contemporary France* (1874–93), and in the twentieth century it underpinned

3

the widely read books of Pierre Gaxotte [35, 7]. With its emphasis on the corrosive role of ideas and the inadequacies of political leadership, it attracted traditionalists who disliked change, detested democracy and despised revolution. For much of the time they represented a small minority, as France became a democracy after 1870 and conservatism later discredited itself by the collaboration of many right-wing intellectuals with the Nazis and the Vichy regime during the Second World War. Yet more recently it has enjoyed a spectacular revival, after the victory of François Mitterrand in the presidential elections of 1981. Mitterrand led a socialist government which included ministers from the French Communist Party, and his decision soon after coming to power to commemorate the bicentenary of the revolution with lavish celebrations in 1989 angered the right, which alleged that the terror was intrinsic to the revolution and directly linked to communist dictatorships of the twentieth century [33]. A distinguished historian of early modern Europe, Pierre Chaunu, revived the ghosts of Burke and Taine to condemn the terror as 'the founding event, in a long and bloody series of events which goes from 1792 to the present day: from intra-French genocide in the catholic Vendée to the Soviet gulag, from the destruction caused by the cultural revolution in communist China to the genocide of the Khmer Rouge in Cambodia'. Using the fashionable imagery of genetics he went on argue that the revolution carried 'in its chromosomes the genetic code of Lenin, Stalin and Pol Pot' [123: *978*]. This was powerful stuff, but several other French historians shared Chaunu's hostility, while outside France it was encouraged by the widespread political welcome given to the collapse of communism in Russia and eastern Europe. This found its most eloquent expression in Simon Schama's best-seller, *Citizens*, published in 1989 [12]. A long narrative history, decorated with superb anecdotal detail, *Citizens* condemned the revolution as an act of collective violence with terror at its very core. 'In some depressingly unavoidable sense,' Schama argued, 'violence *was* the Revolution itself' [12: *xv*].

[ii] The circumstance argument

But was violence the revolution? If the right has always been hostile to the events of 1789–4, the left has consistently been favourable. For liberals who struggled to retain parliamentary monarchy in France after the restoration of the Bourbons in 1815, the revolution had brought the bourgeoisie to power and provided the foundations for parliamentary government [35]. For democrats, or 'radicals', who founded the Third Republic in the 1870s, the radical revolution had provided France with a model for republican democracy. The revolutionary marching song, the *Marseillaise*, was adopted as the country's national anthem in 1879, Bastille Day was made a public holiday in 1880, and the history of the revolution featured strongly in the education provided in the new state primary schools established by the Ferry laws in the early 1880s [40]. Socialist and Marxist historians writing in the first half of the twentieth century added a third layer of support, for although they despised the 'bourgeois' nature of the Third Republic and the revolution, looking forward instead to a proletarian revolution that would create a classless society, they regarded 1789 as a 'progressive' event that had replaced feudalism with a bourgeois social order. That social order was based on industrialisation, which gave rise to a working class, or proletariat, that would soon spearhead a communist revolution to create a classless society. The revolution was therefore a crucial milestone on the rocky road to social utopia [31].

If various traditions on the left favoured the revolution for different reasons, all were united in explaining the violence of terror as the result of 'circumstance' rather than ideology. Far from being intrinsic to the revolution, the terror, according to this view, was forced on to it by the opposition that it faced from counter-revolution and war. The liberal historians of the early nineteenth century contended that it was the only way open to the middle class to protect the gains that it had made from the events of 1789 [38]. According to François Mignet, the revolution was under threat from foreign invasion and civil war, and forced to protect itself: 'Three years of dictatorship may have been a loss for liberty, but not for the revolution. Resistance from within brought about the sovereignty of the multitude, and aggression from without, military domination' [29: *35*]. Much the same approach was adopted by the radical historians of the Third Republic, and is epitomised in the work of Alphonse Aulard, who was the first holder of a chair in the history of the revolution, founded at the Sorbonne by the Paris Municipality in the 1880s [26]. Aulard disliked the violence of the terror and certainly thought that it lasted longer than it should have. Yet he was a committed democrat who admired the revolution for having created France's first republican democracy. He therefore defended terror as legitimate weapon of self-defence against unprovoked attack from foreign powers and counter-revolution. Far from being inherent in the ideology of 1789, it had merely been an improvised response to the threat of destruction, 'formed empirically from day to day out of the elements imposed by the successive necessities of national defence' [2: *357–8*].

Socialist and Marxist historians have since embroidered this line of argument with additional 'circumstances' which reflect their own conviction that social forces are the main driving force in history. For Georges Lefebvre, writing in the 1930s, the terror was not merely a political tactic adopted by the bourgeoisie to save 'their' revolution but the result of deeply felt suspicions among the rural and urban poor of an 'aristocratic plot' to starve them into submission. Plot theory had always existed during the ancien régime to explain setbacks and catastrophes, but it became politicised during the revolution and led to periodic outbursts of violence – or 'punitive reactions' – which politicians diverted into state structures of repression [11]. A similar explanation has been adopted by historians of the urban poor, or 'sans-culottes', who have shown how economic problems and food prices mobilised popular violence behind terror as a means of punishing the rich and market manipulators [78, 103, 164].

[iii] Revisionist historians

The 'circumstance' explanation has always been rejected by conservatives as an attempt to sanitise the work of the guillotine by blaming its victims rather than their killers. 'Circumstance' historians have responded by pointing out that systematic terror, as opposed to sporadic violence, occurred only when military defeat threatened the revolution in 1793, and ended once that threat had disappeared in the summer of 1794. Until recently most academic historians have accepted this argument, and it has dominated school and university texts for much of the twentieth century [30]. Yet more recently it has come under attack from 'revisionist' historians, who protest that it shifts the blame for political violence too readily on to the revolution's opponents and understates the responsibility of the revolutionaries themselves. The roots of revisionism lie in the decline of communism, for during the generation that followed the Second World War the Communist Party was a major political force in France. Decline then set in during the early 1960s as de-Stalinisation in the Soviet Union revealed the darker side of Russian communism and the doctrinal rigidity of the French party alienated most of the younger generation. This shift affected the stranglehold that Marxist historians had on the interpretation of the revolution, for English and American historians had already raised doubts over its bourgeois nature by querying the extent to which class issues caused its outbreak in 1789 [20, 24]. In 1965 a French historian, François Furet, co-authored a history of the revolution which denied that it was a bourgeois revolution against feudalism and argued instead that it was the work of a social elite which included both the wealthier sections of the middle class and the 'feudal' nobility [6]. This in turn led to a reinterpretation of the terror which, instead of explaining it as the result of the 'circumstances' of counter-revolution and war, saw it as the product of a series of political errors which led liberal reform to 'skid' off course into extremism and violence.

This interpretation – sometimes referred to as 'Furet Mark I' – sparked off a bitter argument, for Furet himself had been a member of the French Communist Party in the 1950s and his attack on the Marxist approach appeared to be a settling of scores with former comrades, using the revolution as a weapon of attack. As the debate progressed, however, Furet changed direction under the influence of the ideas of post-structuralism, which emphasised the role of language and concepts in shaping political culture, and picked up substantial support from a number of English and American historians – including Keith Michael Baker and Norman Hampson – who adopted a similarly 'ideas-driven' approach [19, 27, 61]. A revisionist consensus soon emerged which saw ideology rather than social conflict as the key motor behind the radicalism of the revolution, and argued that this ideological radicalism had been present as early as 1789 [5, 19, 17].

The revisionist argument is a complex one, frequently obscured by the use of intricate language and technical terminology [32]. It is a history of words as much as deeds, of ideology as much as action, and not all revisionists use the same bullets or aim at the same targets [37]. Yet their argument essentially revolves around two major points: the political culture of eighteenth-century France; and the influence of Jean-Jacques Rousseau. Furet in particular has argued that the political centralisation carried out during the reign of Louis XIV (1643–1715) had the effect of eliminating representative institutions from political life and forcing the social elite of nobility and bourgeoisie to discuss political issues instead in private gatherings such as reading clubs, literary academies, and Masonic societies. In this rarefied atmosphere the ideas of Rousseau exercised a powerful influence, for in a series of publications ranging from the *Social Contract* (1762) to the *Confessions* (1782) Rousseau had condemned existing society as corrupt and called for a process of social and moral regeneration to recreate a sense of 'virtue', or civic responsibility [23]. This could be carried out only in a society founded on popular sovereignty and governed by direct democracy in which the 'general will' of the community dictated all government decisions [27, 75]. Furet and Hampson have argued that Rousseau's ideas rushed into the vacuum created by the collapse of royal power in 1789, and created the radicalism which made up the real 'mystery' of the revolution. Deputies in the National Assembly promptly set about regenerating France along rational lines, confident that their decisions embodied a 'general will' which, as Rousseau had shown, had to be obeyed by all citizens [54]. Opposition was denounced as conspiracy, genuine political pluralism became impossible, and critics of the Assembly were branded as conspirators and traitors, as politics degenerated into terror [28, 119].

Rousseau's influence destabilised the revolution in another way too, for while he had advocated direct democracy the National Assembly had set up a representative form of government instead, based on an electoral process. Radicals therefore quickly adapted his ideas to subvert representative government during the revolution and justify the use of direct action at times of political crisis. The result was an alliance between radical democrats and the poor which led initially to periodic outbursts of popular violence, and then to the terror of 1793–4. Rousseau's insistence on the need for social and moral regeneration was also a destabilising factor, for it encouraged deputies to abandon moderate reform in favour of radical change, in the mistaken belief that instant 'regeneration' could be achieved by political action [152]. When that perfection failed to materialise, they quickly blamed their failure on counter-revolution and claimed the right to use terror to overcome it. For Furet, therefore, the terror was 'an integral part of revolutionary ideology' from the summer of 1789 until the process burnt itself out with the death of Robespierre in 1794 [27].

This brief outline of the three major arguments over the origins and nature of the terror shows that the differences between the three approaches are political as well as methodological. Conservatives condemn the revolution, revisionists regard its legacy as ambiguous and circumstance historians see it as positive. Both conservatives and revisionists base their interpretation mainly on ideology, while circumstance historians are more concerned with social and political events. Obviously, the revolution and terror still divide historians almost as much as they did the people who lived through the events of the 1790s, and the main difficulty facing the historian is to separate the polemic from the evidence. This is something that the following chapters will attempt to do, picking a path through the historical minefield by tracing the development of the revolution from the initial political breakdown of 1789. For it is obvious, from the historical debate outlined above, that the terror cannot be understood just by looking at the events of 1793 and 1794 in isolation. Instead, it requires us to examine the revolution as a whole to see when reform developed into crisis, and crisis degenerated into terror.

2 Tension or Terror? Reform and Resistance, 1789–91

If terror was an inherent feature of the revolution from the outset, as conservatives and revisionists argue, the years between 1789 and 1791 should provide us with evidence of its origins, its development, and its early impact on revolutionary politics. If, on the other hand, terror only emerged later, in response to the threats posed by counter-revolution and war, then these years should provide evidence of the political crisis that allowed those threats to develop, but not of terror itself. In a short study such as this there is little scope for analysing the events of the early revolution in any detail, but a brief survey of the main reforms, and of the opposition that they encountered, should leave us better placed to evaluate the two conflicting arguments.

[i] Revolutionary reforms

In the autumn of 1788 Louis XVI called an Estates-General to solve the acute financial crisis facing the country. This in itself was an admission of failure, for no such body had met since 1614 because of the steady growth of royal absolutism. Yet failure turned to revolution quite unexpectedly when the elected deputies assembled at Versailles in early May 1789. Those elected to the third estate, who represented the non-privileged sectors of French society, promptly seized the political initiative by refusing to verify their election results until deputies from the other two 'estates', of clergy and nobility, agreed to join them in a single house to debate and vote in common [52]. On 17 June they adopted the title of 'National Assembly', and claimed total control over taxation and legislation in the name of popular sovereignty [63]. Most of the nobility and clergy rejected their action, as did the king, who tried to reassert his authority by convening a special meeting of all three estates on 23 June, at which he proposed a package of moderate reforms. The third estate rejected the package as too moderate and the king retaliated by calling up army regiments to Paris and Versailles with the apparent intention of using force to dissolve the Assembly [81]. The gamble failed, partly because army officers doubted that their troops would obey orders to fire on civilians, and partly because the fall of the Bastille on 14 July meant that the crown could no longer hope to control Paris [56]. Recognising that military action was now impossible without major bloodshed, Louis capitulated and accepted the Assembly's authority. As he did so, urban revolts throughout the country swept royal officials from power and a peasant revolt against feudalism rocked the countryside. In response, the urban bourgeoisie set up local armed units, or National Guards, to maintain order and social discipline [64].

The decisions that shaped the constitution of 1791 were made well before the end of 1789. On 4 August many (although not all) feudal dues were abolished, along with social and regional privilege, transforming subjects into 'citizens' and France into a unitary nation state rather than a collection of historic provinces. Later in the month the Declaration of the Rights of Man listed the political principles that would underpin the new state, and in September two fundamental decisions were made on the shape of the constitution that was to come into effect in 1791 [47]. The first vested political sovereignty in a Legislative Assembly of 745 deputies, and the second limited the king's influence over legislation to a suspensive veto that could last for up to six years [46]. For electoral purposes citizens were divided into three categories, defined by their tax-paying capacity: 'passive' citizens (all adult women and adult men who paid little or no taxes) were full citizens but without voting rights; 'active' citizens (adult males who paid annual taxation worth the equivalent of three days' wages) had the right to vote in primary assemblies; 'eligible' citizens (adult males who paid a substantial amount of annual taxation) could be chosen as deputies and departmental administrators [4].

Administrative and social reforms reflected the same basic ideology of popular sovereignty, as the abolition of provincial privilege led to the restructuring of the country into 83 departments, each of which was subdivided into districts and municipalities. All three levels of local administration were to be run by locally elected councils, instead of the centrally appointed *intendant* of the ancien régime, so decentralising power from the centre to the regions [65]. The legal system was reformed too, as legislation in 1790 set up a criminal court in each department and a civil court in each district, with elected judges, a jury system and a reformed penal code [82]. Economic change followed in the spring of 1791 as the guilds were abolished in the interests of free trade, and three months later journeymen's associations – the equivalent of modern trade unions – were made illegal in the name of individual freedom. Meanwhile political liberty had also been reinforced. Press freedom was listed in the Declaration of the Rights of Man in August 1789, and over the next two years several hundred newspapers and many thousand pamphlets appeared in Paris and the provinces [58]. Political clubs became legal too, many of them springing up in major towns as debating centres for the politically involved middle class. The most influential was the Paris Jacobin club, which began life as a discussion group for Breton deputies in the summer of 1789 and developed into a wider-based political club when the Assembly moved from Versailles to Paris in the late autumn of 1789. By granting affiliation rights to provincial clubs, the Parisian club soon developed into the centre of a national network of 'societies of the friends of the constitution', which numbered over 200 by the spring of 1791 [66].

Religion was buffeted by the wind of change as well, when a commitment to toleration contained in the Declaration of the Rights of Man was confirmed, with Protestants receiving full civil rights in December 1789 and Jews by September 1791. Meanwhile the position of the Catholic Church was affected in other ways, as tithe was abolished in August 1789, and Church land was confiscated by the state in November to resolve its spiralling debt problem [71]. The state accepted responsibility for Church funding but in return the Assembly decided to streamline it in the interests of economy and efficiency. In February 1790 all contemplative religious orders were abolished, and five months later the civil constitution of the clergy reduced the number of bishoprics to one per department, abolished cathedral chapters, and restructured parishes to ensure a more even distribution of population. Bishops and priests were now to be elected by department and district electoral assemblies, with the Pope merely being informed of the results, and new salary scales reduced the income of most bishops while raising that of priests [84].

[ii] Opposition and counter-revolution

These reforms transformed France into a modern parliamentary monarchy within the short space of two years, and were a remarkable achievement which provided an inspiration to reformers and revolutionaries throughout Europe for much of the nineteenth and twentieth centuries [61]. Yet they were also extremely divisive, both within the Assembly and in the country at large. Within the Assembly, opposition first emerged during the autumn of 1789, mainly from members of the nobility and higher clergy, but also from a small number of deputies of the third estate as well. Their opposition focused on the pace and extent of change, and resulted in the formation of two distinct groups, *monarchiens* and *noirs*. The *monarchiens* were constitutional royalists, who admired the British constitutional system and welcomed the Assembly's work in creating parliamentary government. Their main quarrels with the constitutional reforms were over the position of the king, whom they wanted to retain more power in the form of an absolute veto, over the structure of the future Assembly, which they wanted to be bicameral, with an upper house to restrain the radicalism of the elected lower house, and over the position of the Catholic Church, which they regarded as being under threat from the granting of religious toleration to Protestants [60]. To their right lay the reactionaries, or *noirs*, who rejected much of the revolution outright and campaigned for a return to the old structure of the Estates-General, the restoration of feudalism and social privilege, and a complete end to religious toleration [44]. Both groups established their own clubs and newspapers, and during the winter of 1789–90 were able to rally around 400 deputies to their cause, out of a total of a little over 1000, in major voting divisions [74]. Yet that was never enough to challenge seriously the voting strength of the pro-revolutionary 'patriot' majority, and by the summer of 1790 many on the right realised that they were powerless to halt the flow of change [83]. Several *monarchiens* resigned their seats as a result, while many *noirs* either left the Assembly to return home to the provinces, or stayed on to play a deliberately obstructive role in the hope of paralysing the political process and wrecking the revolution.

This had an important effect on the development of revolutionary politics, for it convinced many patriots that there was no chance of meaningful dialogue with a political right that seemed intent on undermining the whole revolutionary achievement. As a result they interpreted every riot and every sign of opposition as the result of counter-revolutionary plots. This obsession with plots was nothing new, for it had been common under the ancien régime for people to blame high food prices on a 'famine plot' by the king and his ministers, and for politicians to blame their difficulties on the 'plots' of their opponents. But in the tense atmosphere of 1789 these 'plots' became integrated into both revolutionary and counter-revolutionary rhetoric, and were blamed by both sides for their setbacks and failures. That process was made easier by the fact that several plots were hatched by the counter-revolutionary right during 1789–90, aimed at spiriting the king away from Paris or at creating serious civil disorder. The decision by right-wing deputies to withdraw from the Assembly and obstruct its business therefore merely confirmed patriot suspicions that conservative criticism was a cover for political subversion, and that suspicion destroyed the chance of a genuinely pluralist political culture developing [86].

Emigration also played a key role in the drift towards political confrontation, for in the autumn of 1789 Louis's younger brother, the Count of Artois, emigrated to Turin, where he set up a counter-revolutionary committee [76]. Over the next two years, several thousand émigrés, mainly drawn from the nobility, clergy, and upper middle class, joined him, and by the summer of 1791 Artois had established a small émigré army of some 6000 men, based in the electorates of Trier and Mainz in the German Rhineland [59]. In military terms the force was tiny, but Artois hoped to attract other European monarchs to his cause with the argument that events in France threatened social and political order in Europe as a whole. Initially he had little success, for few rulers saw the revolution as a threat to their own security and most were happy enough to see France distracted from international power politics by events at home. Even Marie-Antoinette's brother, the Austrian Emperor Leopold II, cold shouldered Artois and the émigrés, partly because he sympathised with several of the Assembly's reforms, but partly too because Marie-Antoinette and Louis XVI urged him to do so. From their point of view Artois' appeals were a threat to their security within France, and a potential challenge to the king's judgement and authority [50, 62].

Left to itself the émigré threat might well have fizzled out, but its effect was magnified by domestic problems within France, and especially in the Rhône valley and Languedoc. In both areas there was a large reservoir of poor nobility who deeply resented the loss of social privilege and feudal dues; but the main impetus to counter-revolutionary involvement came from general Catholic resentment against the granting of toleration to Protestants. Languedoc in particular had a tightly knit Calvinist minority which had survived persecution in the eighteenth century and supported the revolution in 1789. Yet toleration not only legitimised their religion on the same basis as Catholicism, but left them free to contest national and local elections too. When municipal and department elections were held throughout France in the spring of 1790, Protestant successes in a handful of southern departments led to serious riots in Montauban and Nîmes, in which over 300 people – mainly Catholic – died [67, 69]. Local Catholic leaders wasted little time in making contact with Artois, and a large counter-revolutionary demonstration was held by Catholic National Guard units in the Ardèche in August 1790. Plans for an insurrection in Lyon, which would have led to a general uprising in the Rhône valley, were foiled in the following December [80].

Events in the Midi, with their obvious links to subversive émigré activity, convinced patriots that counter-revolutionary plots were both serious and widespread, and during the early spring of 1791 that conviction hardened when an oath of loyalty to the civil constitution of the clergy was applied to priests and bishops. Almost all the bishops and half the parish priests refused to take it, because the civil constitution had not received Papal approval or been submitted for consideration by the French church itself, and the result was a religious schism. The rejection was particularly marked in large areas of the west (the Vendée and Brittany), the north-east, and Alsace and the Midi [84]. Priests who refused the oath became known as 'non-jurors', and violence quickly broke out in many parishes as they were replaced by newly elected 'juror' priests. Parishioners usually rallied to the support of their non-juror priest against the 'intruder', and by the summer of 1791 hostility to religious reform was developing into hostility to the revolution that was enforcing it.

The king's attitude too was problematic, for having lost most of his 'absolute' power during the summer of 1789, he now found himself relegated to the largely honorary position of a constitutional monarch. A quiet and inarticulate man, who rarely expressed himself publicly and found decisions excruciatingly difficult to make, he maintained a facade of cooperation with the Assembly well into 1790 [61]. This in turn encouraged several moderate leaders in the patriot party, who were worried by the growing strength of radicalism, to contact the court with the promise to use their influence to strengthen the king's powers under the new constitution, in return for his willingness to come out in favour of the revolution. Lafayette and Mirabeau both did this in the spring of 1790, and early in 1791 they were followed by an important trio of radical leaders – the so-called 'triumvirate' of Alexandre de Lameth, Adrien Duport, and Antoine Barnave – who had become alarmed at the strength of the radicalism that they had helped to unleash [57, 70]. The king agreed to cooperate, in the apparent hope of regaining much of his former authority, but by the end of 1790 it was obvious that no progress was being made. If anything, the Assembly's mood was becoming more radical. So the king's thoughts turned to the alternative tactic of flight, and on the night of 20–21 June 1791, after months of meticulous planning, the royal family secretly left the Tuileries Palace in a convoy of carriages, bound for the eastern frontier. There the king planned to join up with army units hostile to the revolution, and force the Assembly to revise the constitution radically in his favour.

The 'flight to Varennes' ended in humiliating failure as the carriages fell badly behind schedule and the king was finally recognised and arrested in the small town of Varennes on the night of 21–22 June. The royal family returned to Paris under armed escort four days later, but the alarm bells had rung both at home and abroad. Abroad, Leopold of Austria felt forced to make a gesture of support for the plight of his sister, and issued the Padua Circular on 6 July, calling on other monarchs to help him restore the French monarchy's freedom of action. Six weeks later he met Frederick William II of Prussia, and the two men issued the Declaration of Pillnitz, undertaking to organise military action against France if other European monarchs would join them. Leopold clearly intended this as a bluff, hoping merely to intimidate the Assembly into restoring Louis to the throne, and knowing that European unanimity on an invasion of France was highly improbable; but in France it was widely misread as a threat of imminent invasion and raised political tension [49]. Meanwhile, on the domestic front, once the news of the king's flight broke, the Assembly suspended the king from the throne. Yet most deputies were desperate to retain a constitution that they had worked on already for two years, and were convinced that the alternative of a republic would lead only to complete political democracy, which they were convinced would result in social chaos. So the 'triumvirate' of Duport, Lameth, and Barnave negotiated a deal with the king, offering to persuade the Assembly to modify the constitution in return for his public acceptance of it, and his agreement to cooperate with the revolution in future. The Assembly ratified the deal on 16 July and carried through minor constitutional revisions by early September; Louis formally approved the document on 13 September and was restored to the throne. The future of the constitutional monarchy now seemed secure.

[iii] The radical challenge

Yet behind the patched up compromise public opinion was badly divided. A small group of radical left-wing deputies in the National Assembly, the most prominent of whom was Maximilien Robespierre, had argued from the autumn of 1789 onwards against the franchise provisions of the constitution as a betrayal of popular sovereignty because they imposed a property qualification on voters and deputies [128]. They were also critical of patriot leaders such as Mirabeau and Lafayette, because of their political contacts with the king and court, and their obvious antipathy to democracy. Outside the Assembly these suspicions were supported by a thriving radical newspaper press, and by political clubs in the local government areas of Paris – called 'districts' in 1789–90, and 'sections' from then onwards – which attracted an audience of middle-class activists and radical artisans [51, 77]. The most influential of these was the Cordeliers club on the left bank of the Seine, situated in the heart of the printing and publishing district, but by the spring of 1791 'fraternal' or 'popular' societies had sprung up in other sections too, and a central committee had been formed to coordinate their activity. The concerns of the popular societies were partly economic, for there was a growing unemployment problem in Paris due to the economic disruption caused by the revolution [78]. They were partly religious too, with growing popular hostility towards the Catholic Church and non-juror priests after their rejection of the civil constitution of the clergy. Yet the main emphasis was political. Opposition to the franchise provisions of the constitution had grown rather than diminished over the 18 months since the autumn of 1789, while there was growing popular hostility to the king and queen because of their suspected opposition to the revolution. By the spring of 1791, Louis was being portrayed in popular cartoons as

17

an overweight pig, wallowing in his own filth. Marie-Antoinette was variously portrayed as a mutant hyena or hideous pea-hen with a voracious sexual appetite allied to a hatred of the French which stemmed from her Austrian origins [45].

The popular societies exploded into action after the flight to Varennes. The Cordeliers club demanded a democratic referendum on the future of the monarchy, and on 17 July a petition for a republic was opened for signatures on the field of the Champ de Mars in central Paris, the site of the present Eiffel Tower [77]. However, the Assembly's decision to reinstate the king had been made the previous day, and as huge crowds gathered at the Champ de Mars to sign the petition, the Paris Municipality proclaimed martial law and sent in the National Guard to restore order. In the fighting that followed, several demonstrators were killed and more than 200 radicals arrested [78]. The 'massacre of the Champ de Mars', as the event came to be known, silenced the radical movement in the short term, and gave the Assembly valuable breathing space in which to revise the constitution. Yet in the longer term it strengthened popular alienation from the constitution by revealing the gap between the constitutional liberalism of the middle class and the democratic aspirations of the radical left. Unlike counter-revolutionaries, Parisian radicals did not want to overthrow the constitution and return to the ancien régime; but they did want the constitution democratised and were rapidly becoming more republican in their views.

[iv] Crisis or terror?

By the autumn of 1791 the Assembly had achieved its aim of providing France with a written constitution, embodying a wide range of social and religious reforms. Yet reform had been bought at a price. On the right, the king was clearly unhappy with the loss of his traditional power, the émigrés had voted with their feet, and the civil constitution of the clergy had pushed large sections of the rural population into the counter-revolutionary camp. On the left, radicals distrusted the king, disliked the constitution, and were deeply sceptical of the patriot politicians who had drafted it. While the right wanted the revolution reversed, radicals wanted France to develop into a republican democracy. Do these divisions mark the beginning of the terror, or are they just the growing pains of a new political system? We saw in the previous chapter that right-wing historians have attributed the terror to the political inexperience and abstract rationalism of the revolution's early stages. There is no evidence from the events of 1789 to 1791 to support this diagnosis, for most deputies had been closely involved in politics before the revolution. Almost a third had held office in the administrative and judicial institutions of the old regime, while others were members of trade guilds, provincial academies, Masonic lodges or chambers of commerce, where the process of discussion, debate, and compromise was commonplace [83, 79]. Neither is it accurate to describe their approach to politics as dominated by abstract reason. Instead, their libraries and the letters that they wrote home to their family or constituents reveal a broad cultural background, in which modern science, classical learning, geography, literature, and politics all played an important part. No single conceptual framework dominated their minds, and they were certainly not the rationalist robots of a one-dimensional Enlightenment [85].

Evidence of their administrative experience and varied cultural background weakens the revisionist case too, which also argues that the middle class lacked political experience and was attracted by abstract rationalism. It also undermines the emphasis placed by Furet and Hampson on the influence of Rousseau, for although Rousseau had become a cult figure during the 1780s, it was more for his educational and autobiographical writings than for his political views [53]. Some prominent deputies in 1789, like the Abbé Sieyès, had read the *Social Contract* and used Rousseau's concepts in the debates over constitutional change, but they were a tiny minority, and if concepts such as 'general will' and 'popular sovereignty' cropped up in debate it was more because they were part of the political vocabulary of the age than because deputies were working to a specifically Rousseauist agenda. More deputies referred to history or to God when writing to their constituents than referred to reason, the general will, or Rousseau [85]. Indeed, in key areas of legislation such as religious reform and the civil constitution of the clergy, Voltaire's anticlericalism clearly carried more weight than Rousseau's deism.

The real problem during these early years lay less in ideological radicalism than in the bitter confrontation that developed between the revolution and its opponents. In most modern political systems conflict is handled by the formation of political parties, acceptance of the principle of majority voting, and consensus on the fundamental values of the political system. That never happened in the revolution,

19

because France lacked a parliamentary tradition, and because the right refused to recognise the legitimacy of revolutionary change [44]. As a result, the gap between left and right quickly became unbridgeable, and politics polarised. Despite that polarisation the Assembly's approach to reform remained impressively pluralistic. In the teeth of a vociferous right-wing press which supported émigré activity and counter-revolutionary violence, press legislation between 1789 and 1791 remained remarkably liberal, maintaining the principle of press freedom embedded in the Declaration of the Rights of Man, and allowing newspapers of both the radical left and the reactionary right to flourish. Freedom of assembly allowed clubs from both sides of the political divide to thrive, and a recent study has shown that the new court system established in 1790 dealt with political cases in a remarkably even-handed manner. The only person executed for a political crime before 1792 was the Marquis de Favras, decapitated in February 1790 for plotting to kidnap the king in the cause of counter-revolution [82]. France was certainly a divided country, but intolerance came from the right more than from the left, and there was no indication yet of systematic political terror. That was to come only with war [43].

3   From Crisis to Terror: A Divided Republic, 1791–3

Just how the revolution would have evolved if war had not intervened in the spring of 1792 is one of history's elusive 'might-have-beens'; but the fact is that war did, and by the late summer of 1792 the constitution had collapsed and over 2000 people had been killed on the streets of Paris. In September 1792, a democratic republic was proclaimed and a National Convention elected to draft a new constitution. Yet by the following spring, war against Austria had escalated into a general European conflict, and counter-revolution had erupted in the Vendée, in the west of France. As the crisis deepened, politicians in the Convention took emergency measures to centralise government, strengthen the armies, and clamp down on political dissent. Yet, as they did so, a power struggle erupted within their ranks between two opposing groups, Girondins and Mountain, which culminated the expulsion and arrest of the Girondins on 2 June 1793. That event marked a crucial stage in the transition from political normality to terror, for not only had war undermined the constitution and provoked civil war, but it now threatened the very ideals of freedom so central to the events of 1789. Royalists had been swept from politics in August 1792, and now moderate republicans shared their fate. The revolution was devouring not just its opponents but its supporters as well, and the country was teetering on the edge of the terror. The three main features of this crucial transition were the decision to launch war in the spring of 1792, the collapse of the constitution in the summer, and the political struggle between Girondins and Mountain from the winter of 1792 through to the spring of 1793. Between them they changed the politics and the course of the revolution.

[i] The declaration of war

On 22 May 1790 the National Assembly had solemnly renounced the idea of offensive war, declaring that the French people 'would never use its power against the liberty of any people'. Less than two years later, on 20 April 1792, its successor, the Legislative Assembly, declared war on Austria with only seven dissenting votes, and 23 years of continuous military conflict followed. It was once argued that war was caused by foreign hostility to the revolution, but most historians now argue that the Legislative Assembly brought the problem on its own head through a combination of political miscalculation and clumsy diplomacy [49]. Part of the clumsiness stemmed from the fact that all its deputies were new to national politics, for in May 1791 the National Assembly had passed a self-denying ordinance on its own members, in the belief that new faces would provide the country with a fresh start. Yet this meant that most of them lacked the national experience that their predecessors had built up over the previous two years, and brought to Paris instead the concerns that they had encountered as local administrators at departmental level. These were essentially the religious problems caused by the civil constitution of the clergy and the threat to the revolution posed by the émigrés [72, 73]. Almost immediately they took action against both. On 9 November 1791 they decreed that émigrés who failed to return to France before the end of the year would be treated as traitors and lose their property, and later in the month they voted for non-juror priests to be put under house arrest in cases where political violence broke out in their parish.

The king vetoed both decrees, which increased popular suspicion over his alleged loyalty to the revolution, but the Assembly quickly turned its attention from domestic to international politics under the influence of a small group of deputies who rose to prominence through their oratory and journalism. Known to contemporaries as the 'brissotins', because many were associated with the journalist and deputy Jacques-Pierre Brissot, they are better known to history as the 'Girondins' because several came from the department of the Gironde in the south-west of France [156, 167]. The Girondins believed that the revolution's difficulties could be solved by striking at the émigrés, and at Austria, which had engineered the Declaration of Pillnitz after the flight to Varennes. In late November they persuaded the Assembly to call on the king formally to warn the electors of Trier and Mainz that they faced military invasion unless they expelled the émigré armies from their territories. The king readily agreed, hoping that war would prove to be a disaster, but both electors promptly complied with his demand, and the crisis seemed to pass [80]. However, Leopold II then intervened to warn that Austria would protect both states against a French attack. This merely convinced the Girondins that the threat contained in the Declaration of Pillnitz remained active, and that Austria was the real motivating force behind counter-revolution. On 24 January 1792, the Assembly therefore called on Leopold to confirm that the alliance between the two countries, which dated back to 1756, still stood, but the Austrian reply in mid-February was deliberately aggressive. Louis XVI then encouraged the slide towards war by appointing a new ministry in early March, under an experienced army general, Dumouriez, which included several friends and colleagues of the Girondins [50]. Six weeks later the Assembly declared war.

Two themes played an important role in the Girondin war campaign: the dream of a European-wide revolution, and a profound suspicion that counter-revolutionaries were plotting to restore the ancien régime. War was the panacea for both, for the Girondins argued that it would encourage people throughout Europe to rise up in support of the revolution, and simultaneously force the king to make the choice between acceptance of the revolution or abdication. Supporters of counter-revolution within France would suffer too, for one of the Girondins in the Assembly, Elie Guadet, urged: 'Let us mark out a place in advance for traitors, and let that place be the scaffold'. The Girondins specialised in extravagant rhetoric, and perhaps it would be unwise to take these words – and others like them – entirely at face value. Yet the threat to regard political opponents and traitors shows the way in which Girondin enthusiasm, and their extravagant rhetoric, was taking them away from the liberal tolerance of 1789. The Girondins had taken the first step on the path to a terror that within 18 months was to lead to their own destruction [50].

[ii] The collapse of the constitution and the 'first terror'

The impact of war was quickly felt, for initial skirmishes between French and Austrian troops on the Belgian border in late April 1792 ended in a chaotic French retreat. By mid-May Prussia had joined

Austria in the conflict, and French generals were calling for a negotiated truce. The Girondins reacted angrily to the call, blaming their setbacks on the catch-all 'problem' of counter-revolutionary conspiracy rather than on their own military misjudgement, and persuaded the Assembly to counteract the conspiracy by ordering the deportation of non-juror priests from areas of disturbances, and by establishing a camp of 20 000 National Guards on the edge Paris to protect the capital against the Austro-Prussian advance. The king vetoed both decrees, and when the Girondin ministers protested, dismissed them from office on 13 June. Now the Girondins faced their moment of truth, for they had always argued war would enable the revolution to isolate its traitors, and the logic of that argument now pointed to action against the king.

The possibility for action was certainly there, for war propaganda had whipped up political enthusiasm in Paris among artisans and labourers who had been largely excluded from politics by the franchise provisions of the constitution. They had adopted the title of 'sans-culottes', a phrase initially thrown at them as an insult because they wore labourers' trousers rather than the breeches of the aristocracy, and had retained the hostility towards the king evident already at the time of the massacre of the Champ de Mars. On 20 June they organised a mass march to the Assembly to protest against the Girondins' dismissal, which overflowed into the Tuileries Palace, where they paraded through the royal apartments, calling on the king to restore the ministers and withdraw his veto [78]. The king refused, confident that complete collapse was only weeks away, and during the month of July most sans-culottes in the Paris sections began holding daily meetings to keep in touch with the developing crisis. Many sections allowed in 'passive' citizens who had been deprived of the vote under the 1791 constitution, and by the end of July they were joined by hundreds of provincial National Guards, known as *fédérés*, who arrived in Paris to take part in the celebrations for the third anniversary of the fall of the Bastille [147].

The Girondins could have used sans-culotte and *fédéré* pressure to persuade the king to back down, or to force an abdication. Yet most deputies in the Assembly opposed that kind of unconstitutional action, and the Girondins themselves held back, alarmed by the strength and radicalism of sans-culotte agitation [174]. Instead, they made secret contact with the king in the hope of negotiating themselves back into ministerial office, but this left a political vacuum on the left into which Maximilien Robespierre and the radical wing of the Jacobin club stepped. Robespierre was not a member of the Legislative Assembly because of the self-denying ordinance on deputies in the Constituent Assembly, but he had remained active in the Jacobin club during the winter of 1791–2, where he had vehemently opposed the Girondin war campaign on the grounds that it would aggravate the revolution's problems rather than solve them. Now that war had arrived he argued that the political crisis demanded radical solutions and, in the Jacobin club in late July, he stated that 'the state must be saved by whatever means, and the only unconstitutional acts are those which lead to its ruin' [128: *113*]. The unconstitutional act was not long in coming, for on 3 August, 47 of the 48 Paris sections gave an ultimatum to the Assembly to remove the king. When it refused, sans-culottes and *fédérés* then attacked the Tuileries Palace in the early morning of 10 August, forcing it to suspend him from power. Once that vote had been taken the constitution itself was invalid, and the Assembly ordered elections for a National Convention to draft a new constitution. In the meantime, until the elections had been completed, the Legislative Assembly limped on for another six weeks, with the Girondin ministers recalled to provide a provisional government [147]. Yet the Assembly's authority lay in ruins, for its failure to take action against the king during June and July had left the way open for the sans-culottes to use violence in August instead. The slide from constitutional politics to terror had begun.

The insurrection of 10 August 1792 was the bloodiest day of the revolution so far, leaving some 800 of the Swiss guards defending the palace, and 376 of their attackers, dead or wounded. Yet worse was to come during the next six weeks as the so-called 'first terror' developed in both Paris and the provinces. On 17 August the Paris Commune, the capital's municipal government whose personnel had been radically reshuffled in the course of the 10 August insurrection, persuaded the Assembly to set up a political court, the 'court of 17 August', to try those involved in the defence of the Tuileries Palace. The court carried out its first execution eight days later. A week later the advancing Prussians captured the key fortress of Longwy in their advance on Paris, and the Commune promptly ordered the arrest of political suspects, and ordered adult males to join the army as volunteers. Rumours then spread that prisoners in Parisian jails were plotting to break out while the volunteers were away at the front, to murder women and children, and hand the city over to the Prussians.

As a result, when news arrived on 2 September that the Prussians had advanced past the last major fortress protecting Paris, Verdun, panic exploded into violence. A crowd intercepted a wagon load of prisoners on their way across Paris to the Abbaye prison, and massacred them on the spot. Groups of sans-culottes then invaded prisons, and set up impromptu courts to dispense 'revolutionary' justice. In the 'September massacres' which followed, between 1100 and 1300 prisoners were hacked or bludgeoned to death in five days of brutal violence, usually after summary 'trials' in prison courtyards or on the streets. Among the dead were some 200 priests, and a number of prominent royalists, but the vast majority were common criminals suspected of collusion with the counter-revolution [100]. The ferocity of the massacres shocked deputies, but there was little that they could do without turning on the very people whose manpower was essential for the defence of Paris. They therefore accepted the slaughter as a regrettable necessity, but when news later leaked out that the Paris Commune's watch committee, of which Robespierre was a member, had tried to have Brissot and Roland arrested on the day that the massacres started, the Girondins promptly denounced the massacres, and accused Jacobins and sans-culottes of planning to set up a dictatorship [106].

[iii] Gironde against Mountain

The animosity between the Girondins and Jacobins dominated the next stage in the transition towards the full-blown terror of 1793–4. Initially its impact was muffled by a change in military fortunes, for on 20 September the French army defeated the Prussians at the battle of Valmy, some 200 kilometres to the east of Paris, and both the Austrian and Prussian armies began to retreat. By the end of the year French armies had occupied Belgium and the Rhineland, Savoy had been annexed, and Girondin dreams of a European-scale revolution seemed on the verge of realisation. On 19 November the National Convention promised 'assistance and fraternity' to all oppressed peoples wishing 'to recover their liberty', and before the end of the year it had pledged to destroy feudalism wherever its armies went [49].

Yet fraternity was not on the domestic agenda of the Convention when it took over from the Legislative Assembly in late September. The Girondins were well placed to dominate it and impose their own political views, for they still held the main ministerial posts and had a solid core of just over 170 deputies (out of a total of 745) committed to them [68, 132]. The Jacobins – who now took on the name of the 'Mountain' because they sat in the upper rows of the Convention hall – probably had the support of more deputies, but a large middle group, called the 'Plain', supported the Girondins because of their fear of Jacobin radicalism and detestation of the violence of the September massacres [156, 167]. With intelligent tactics the Girondins could have achieved their two main political aims of establishing a moderate republic and carrying on a war of liberation in Europe with the support of the Plain. But they squandered their advantage by a series of tactical blunders [8]. The most serious of these occurred over the trial of the king. Louis had been imprisoned since 10 August, but the Convention now had to decide on his fate. Most Girondins wanted him to remain behind bars as a possible bargaining counter in future peace negotiations. The Mountain, on the other hand, argued that the people had judged him a traitor by its insurrection on 10 August, and the Convention's task was merely to order his execution. When the issue was debated in the second half of November, most deputies came round to the Mountain's view that the king had to die, but wanted death to be administered through some form of trial [173]. In early December the Convention therefore voted to transform itself into a court for the purpose of trying the king; he was duly provided with defence lawyers, and proceedings began on 10 December. A month later, in a series of dramatic votes, Louis was found guilty of treason, and sentenced to death without the right of appeal. On the morning of 21 January 1793 he was guillotined on the Place de la Révolution (now the Place de la Concorde) in central Paris, in front of a large crowd which sang the new revolutionary anthem, the *Marseillaise*. His head and body were then placed in an open coffin, covered with quicklime to ensure rapid decomposition, and buried in an unmarked grave in the Madeleine cemetery [136].

The king's execution was an act of political justice which deliberately side-stepped the normal structures of the legal system, and this has prompted some historians to argue that it marked the beginning of the terror. Yet that probably exaggerates its importance, for his case was clearly exceptional (the only recent precedent in European history was the execution of Charles I in England in 1649), and his death was not followed by any immediate sequel of political executions [115, 172]. Instead, its most important contribution to the terror lay in its political consequences, for most Girondins had opposed the trial in the first place, and fought had hard against the imposition of the death penalty, first by voting against it, and then by calling a referendum on the issue. Their failure showed that the balance of power within the Convention was swinging away from them, as deputies of the Plain sided with the Mountain over the issue, and it led to the inevitable accusations that, behind their republican exterior, the Girondins remained unreconstructed crypto-royalists, whose commitment to a new republic was fraudulent [173].

Those suspicions increased in the spring of 1793, when the military successes of late 1792 boomeranged. Britain and Holland had become alarmed by the French conquest of Belgium, and in early February the Convention pre-emptively declared war on both. Within little more than a month Britain had pulled together a military alliance, the First Coalition, which united most of the major European states against the revolution. French armies under General Dumouriez were driven out of Holland in late February, and roundly defeated in Belgium during March. Meanwhile, another army, under Custine, was forced to retreat in the German Rhineland. Dumouriez promptly blamed the Convention for his defeats, and tried to persuade his troops to march on Paris to carry out a coup d'état; but they refused, and he was forced to cross enemy lines to surrender to the Austrians instead. Meanwhile, in an attempt to stop the rot, the Convention ordered the conscription of 300 000 extra men to bolster troop numbers; but the levy caused violent resistance in several parts of the country. In the west, in four departments (the Vendée, the Deux-Sèvres, the Maine-et-Loire, and the Sarthe), it detonated a civil war as artisans and peasants over a wide area adopted guerrilla tactics to defy conscription and attack towns where revolutionary administration was based [158]. Administrators, National Guards and local Jacobins were murdered and, to symbolise their rejection of the revolution and all its works, the Vendéan rebels began to wear sacred hearts and the royalist white cockade [157].

The causes of the Vendée revolt were more complex than the symbols of church and king might suggest. Land hunger was one cause, for the local peasantry had hoped to be able to buy Catholic Church land when it had been put on sale from 1790 onwards, but quickly found themselves outbid by wealthy middle-class purchasers from nearby towns. There was resentment too against the way in which tax levels in the area had risen since 1789, and against the fact that the urban middle class had dominated elections to the new administrative bodies set up by reforms in local government since 1790 [170]. Religion acted as a rallying point for mounting opposition to the revolution, as over 90 per cent of the priests in the area had rejected the civil constitution of the clergy, and military conscription then proved to be the final straw [168]. Yet counter-revolution and the catastrophic defeats in Belgium now convinced many deputies that the very survival of the revolution was at stake. Rather than risk a return to the bloody chaos of the September massacres, with Parisian radicals taking the law into their own hands, the Convention quickly set up a political machinery of terror in an attempt to pre-empt popular violence. On 10 March 1793 it established a revolutionary tribunal in Paris to try cases of treason and counter-revolution. Made up of five judges and 12 jurors, its verdicts were to be carried out within 24 hours, with no right of appeal [121, 124]. On 19 March it also ordered armed rebels to be executed within 24 hours of their capture, and two days later it ordered surveillance committees to be elected in every village and town, to register foreigners and monitor their activities [162]. On 29 March a press law stipulated the death penalty for journalists or authors who supported the monarchy, while political and administrative structures were tightened up too, to counteract civil war and reinforce the war effort. On 10 March, 82 deputies were sent out to the provinces as representatives on mission to supervise both recruitment and the war effort. On 6 April a Committee of Public Safety of nine deputies (later expanded to 12) was established, with its members to be elected every month by the Convention from within its own ranks. Its role was to supervise the work of ministers, tighten up administration, and coordinate military activity [93, 154].

The March–April crisis put the machinery of terror into place and reflected the Mountain's growing influence in the Convention. Yet the Girondins had doggedly opposed much of the legislation, and in mid-April they fought back, helped by the way in which the Mountain's voting strength in the Convention was temporarily weakened by the departure of many of its deputies to the provinces as representatives on mission to supervise recruitment. On 12 April they had the radical journalist Marat sent before the revolutionary tribunal for signing a Jacobin club circular which called on voters to recall Girondin deputies who had opposed the king's execution [122]. When he was acquitted, they then took on the Paris Commune, which was sympathetic to the Mountain, persuading the Convention in late May to set up a Commission of Twelve to investigate its political activities. The Commission promptly arrested several of the Commune's members, including another radical journalist, Hébert, whose *Père Duchesne* had a sizeable sans-culotte readership. Equally worrying from the Jacobin point of view was a moderate backlash in the provinces. In both Lyon and Marseille, Jacobin municipalities were overthrown in May by moderates who had few direct links with the Girondins, but who shared their distaste for Jacobinism and political radicalism [110, 161].

The Girondin fight back was nevertheless ended by sans-culotte violence. After the September massacres, the Parisian sans-culottes had retreated into the political background as the crisis eased; but in the spring of 1793 economic and political problems propelled them back to centre stage. The Convention financed war by printing more paper money, or *assignats*, but over-issue caused their worth to plummet to less than 30 per cent of their face value by March 1793, causing problems for sans-culottes, who were mostly paid in them. At the same time a slave revolt in the French Caribbean islands had disrupted coffee and sugar supplies, forcing their prices up to more than double the normal value [78]. On 25–26 February sans-culotte riots had broken out, directed against wholesale merchants, in which a group of activists called the Enragés played a leading role. One of their leaders, a radical priest called Jacques Roux, called for the execution of hoarders and speculators, and the introduction of price controls on basic commodities [160]. Both the Girondins and the Mountain had always defended the principle of the free market economy, but during March and April the Mountain modified its view, and on 4 May persuaded the Convention to impose a national maximum on grain prices.

This economic alliance between the Mountain and the sans-culottes was reinforced by a political one. On the night of 9–10 March, as the first news of defeats in Belgium trickled through, a small group of Enragés and sans-culottes had smashed the presses of leading Girondin newspapers, and attempted to start an insurrection. That failed, but five weeks later, on 15 April, a majority of the Paris sections petitioned the Convention to remove 22 Girondin deputies. When the Convention refused, the Paris Commune took on the task of planning an insurrection, and leaders of the Mountain, including Robespierre, made it clear that they would not intervene. On 2 June the Convention was finally surrounded by 70 000 National Guards from the Paris sections, demanding the arrest of the Girondin leadership. After a brief attempt at resistance, deputies gave way and placed 29 Girondins – including both deputies and former ministers – under house arrest [163].

[iv] On the edge of terror

The removal of the Girondins was the first parliamentary purge of the revolution. By June 1793 the king was dead, the constitution defunct, and the foundations of the terror had been laid by political centralisation, the creation of the revolutionary tribunal, and the emergence of a tactical alliance between Jacobins and sans-culottes. Parliamentary government was under threat, and war had played a major part in its difficulties, for although twentieth-century experience suggests that war can unite people in the common cause of patriotism, patriotism in France in 1792–3 was not a common cause. The revolution had divided political opinion before 1792, and war had widened those divisions subsequently. The Girondins, who bear the main responsibility for war, made the fatal miscalculation that it was perfectly compatible with normal politics and a free market economy. The Jacobin deputies of the Mountain, on the other hand, had come round to the view that crises required emergency solutions, and that the revolution's survival demanded the temporary sacrifice of some of its principles. Their tactical alliance with the sans-culottes provided that emergency solution, and a combination of war and political conflict therefore played a major role in pushing the revolution from crisis to terror. Yet ideology had a role to play too, for during their war campaign in the winter of 1791–2 the Girondins had exploited a fear of plots and conspiracies that had haunted revolutionaries since 1789. It was they who had first aired the view that the revolution's opponents were traitors who deserved the guillotine, and by the spring of 1793 their rhetoric had boomeranged. Jacobins and sans-culottes now interpreted Girondin opposition to the king's removal in the summer of 1792 and to his execution in the following January as evidence of crypto-royalism and treason. That same fear of treason resurfaced in the spring of 1793 to 'explain' the military defeats in Belgium and counter-revolution in the Vendée. Royalist plots existed, and the defection of Dumouriez to the Austrians in early April was a particularly spectacular example of treason. Yet the Girondins, for all their faults and political errors, were guilty of neither plots nor treason. Their real

31

'crimes' were political incompetence and a reluctance to accept popular democracy. In the context of 1793 this was enough to convince their opponents that they were guilty of treason. That conviction was incorrect, but the deeply held belief that the revolution was lost if the Girondins retained their political influence was not. The heady freedom of 1789 had degenerated into a murky hangover of suspicion by the summer of 1793, and the consequences of the mood swing were soon to make themselves felt.

4 The Rise of the Committee of Public Safety: June–December 1793

By the summer of 1793 the revolution was under attack on three fronts. The first two of these were war against the First Coalition and civil war in the Vendée, both of which called for sustained military effort and for reinforcement of the kind of government centralisation that had been initiated in March and April. The third came from its own supporters, for the sans-culottes who had carried out the Girondin purge on 2 June had their own aims and objectives. Like the Jacobins, they wanted military victory and an end to civil war, but they had a social and political vision of the revolution, too, that victory was designed to protect. Their social demands included price controls on basic foodstuffs to reduce hardship for the poor, and the setting up of a civilian 'revolutionary army' to search rural areas in search of food and food hoarders. Their political demands included the intensified use of the guillotine against counter-revolutionaries, the removal of nobles from public office, and the devolution of more power to sections and municipalities to ensure that the people could exercise their sovereignty by taking a more direct role in their own political destiny. Their cooperation with Jacobin politicians was therefore based on fragile foundations. Both wanted to 'save' the revolution by defeating its enemies, but they differed in their definitions of what the revolution ultimately meant. Jacobins wanted a centralised democracy, based on elections and representative government, governing a society with a free market economy in which the state intervened to help the poor and needy. Sans-culottes, on the other hand, wanted a direct democracy that would enable people to participate directly in the political process, and a controlled social order in which government would enforce a 'moral economy' to ensure that goods were sold at a 'just price' within reach of ordinary people. The result of these conflicting aims was a seesaw political struggle for the next six months, as the Convention grappled with the challenges of war and civil war at the same time as it struggled to control the demands of its sans-culotte allies. By the end of 1793 it had achieved victory in both and the Committee of Public Safety had emerged as the effective head of a centralised government machine. But the victory was far from bloodless, for by then over 3000 people a month were being executed for their political 'crime' of opposition to the republic.

[i] Civil war and foreign invasion

In the immediate aftermath of the Girondin purge the Convention tried to head off potential opposition by downplaying its impact on political life. The Girondin deputies were placed under house arrest rather than being imprisoned, and as proof of its commitment to constitutionalism the Convention pressed on with finalising the text of the constitution that it had been elected to draw up some nine months previously. The so-called 'constitution of 1793' was completed by the end of June and was an extremely democratic document which provided for universal male suffrage, annual elections to a single-house parliament, and the use of referenda for major legislation. It was put to a plebiscite during July, and ratified by an overwhelming majority, but it turned out to be a largely a paper exercise, as only a minority of the population voted and the war crisis meant that it stood no chance of immediate implementation [105]. Instead, survival remained the major concern as, during June and July, Austrian armies pushed into northern France, the Prussians threatened Alsace, and Spanish troops crossed the Pyrenees to surround Perpignan. In the Vendée rebels captured Angers and Saumur during June, almost took Nantes at the end of the month, and routed a government army at Châtillon on 5 July.

The doomsday scenario was made still gloomier by the outbreak of a 'federalist' revolt in the provinces, for when news of the Girondin arrests reached Lyon and Marseille in early June, moderates in both cities denounced it as unconstitutional and rejected the Convention's authority [111, 161]. Several other cities in the Midi followed suit, while in the north-west Caen became the centre of resistance for Normandy and Brittany [116, 131]. By late June 49 departments had thrown in their lot with the revolt – although many never took their protest beyond the verbal stage – and in mid-July the Mediterranean port of Toulon joined too [104]. Faced with the prospect of an extra civil war to add to its problems in the Vendée, the Convention initially tried to negotiate its way out of trouble; but the major rebel towns refused to compromise and called instead for an alternative Convention to meet in the town of Bourges, in central France. Several also began raising armies to march on Paris to restore 'legitimate' government, while in Lyon, Toulon, and Marseille, federalist authorities set up revolutionary courts which tried and guillotined local Jacobin leaders.

In denouncing the revolt as 'federalist', the Convention claimed that the rebels were cooperating with royalists to smash the revolution, and fragment the country into small 'federal' units. But this was sheer propaganda, for in fact the revolt's aims were quite different [116]. Despite the fact that many royalists joined the revolt once it had started, and emerged as its military leaders in Lyon and Marseille, most 'federalists' were in fact moderate republicans who opposed counter-revolution but also objected to Jacobin arrogance towards the principle of parliamentary sovereignty epitomised in Parisian violence and the Girondin arrests [109]. Their problem was that their action, taken at a time of obvious national crisis, left them wide open to the charge of treason, and they compounded that problem by failing to organise their resistance in any coordinated way. The attempts to convoke the alternative Convention at Bourges never materialised, and the federalist armies proved lamentably ineffective. In Marseille over 4000 men were recruited, who advanced up the Rhône valley towards Paris in early July, but were defeated at Pont-Saint-Esprit on 14 July, and fell back on Marseille in disarray. The Normandy army was routed at Pacy-sur-Eure on 13 July, and the Bordeaux army, which attracted less than 400 recruits, broke up in drunken disarray before it even left the department of the Gironde.

Yet the fact of resistance and the raising of federalist armies quickly changed the Convention's initial policy towards both federalism and the Vendée from conciliation into coercion. On 14 July it ordered a detachment of the army of the Alps to crush the revolt in Lyon, and on 1 August reinforced its manpower in the Vendée by sending an army released by the Prussians from the siege of Mainz to wage total war. Crops were to be destroyed, forests burnt, women and children deported to the interior, and the rebels themselves killed 'to extirpate the two greatest diseases from which nations suffer, religious fanaticism and royalist superstition' [145: *196*]. The same change from conciliation to coercion lay behind its decision on 10 July to reshuffle the membership of the Committee of Public Safety. On 10 July Danton and fellow moderates were replaced by radicals who were ready to enforce more hard-line policies. Maximilien Robespierre was added on 27 July, and two army officers with experience in military affairs, Lazare Carnot and Prieur de la Côte d'Or, in mid-August [154].

[ii] The sans-culotte challenge

The swing to coercion was reinforced by sans-culotte pressure, for during June and July growing food shortages had aggravated sans-culotte demands for vigorous action to improve supplies and control prices. A leading role in the agitation was taken by the Enragés, who had risen to prominence since the food riots in February, and in late June their leader, Jacques Roux, led a deputation to the Convention to demand the death penalty for speculators and hoarders. He was shouted down and humiliated then, but the political mood changed on the evening of 13 July when the radical journalist, Marat, was assassinated while taking his regular medicinal bath. He was buried three days later, after his embalmed body had been carried in a solemn procession through the streets of Paris with the knife wound exposed for all to see. His assassin, a young royalist woman from Normandy, Charlotte Corday d'Armont, who had murdered him because of her hatred of Jacobinism, was guillotined the next day, dressed in the red cloak reserved for political assassins [125]. Yet, far from destroying Jacobinism as Corday had hoped, the effect of Marat's murder was to accelerate the slide towards extremism, as a secular cult sprang up among sans-culottes to commemorate his role in the revolution as a 'patriotic martyr' [165]. More ominously, Jacques Roux and a fellow Enragé, Théophile Leclerc, returned to the offensive with their own 'continuations' of his newspaper, the *Publiciste de la République* and the *Ami du Peuple*, in which they denounced the Convention's failure to tackle counter-revolution adequately, and called for a full enforcement of terror. This prompted another influential journalist, Hébert, to radicalise his *Père Duchesne* for fear of losing his sans-culotte readership. With food supplies to Paris almost drying up because of the disruption caused by civil war, Hébert called for price controls, and the use of the guillotine against hoarders and speculators. That spelled danger for the Convention, for the *Père Duchesne* was popular with the sans-culottes, and Hébert an influential figure in both the Cordelier and Jacobin clubs [166].

Deputies therefore quickly conceded some of the sans-culotte demands. On 26 July the hoarding of basic foodstuffs was made a capital offence, and on 9 August a decree ordered the setting up of public granaries in every district so that grain could be bought in when prices were low, and sold off when prices were high, in an attempt to even out price variations. On 23 August, to reinforce the war effort, the *levée en masse* was passed in response to repeated sans-culotte demands. The sans-culottes had in fact wanted a spontaneous mobilisation of the entire population to drive the enemy out by sheer weight of numbers, but this would have caused chaos, and instead the Convention declared the entire male population liable for requisition for the war effort, but restricted its practical effects to single men between the ages of 18 and 25. They were ordered into the army immediately, and by the end of the year the army's total strength had risen from just under half a million to over 800 000 [89]. But all these measures needed time to work, and time was not on the Convention's side. On 2 September news filtered through to Paris that federalist authorities in the port of Toulon had handed the city over to a British fleet under Admiral Hood, and declared their allegiance Louis XVI's son and heir, Louis XVII. This spectacular treason heightened the atmosphere of political tension, and on 4 September a sans-culotte demonstration for higher wages and better food supplies was held outside the town hall in Paris. On the following day they directed their frustration towards the Convention, with a mass march that ended up with an invasion of the Convention's meeting hall. Sans-culotte leaders demanded the immediate arrest of political suspects and the creation of a 'revolutionary army' to search the surrounding countryside for food. Rather than risk a parliamentary purge, deputies conceded both points, and also voted two prominent radical deputies on to the Committee of Public Safety – Collot d'Herbois and Billaud-Varenne – to strengthen sans-culotte confidence [99, 144].

The events of 5 September provided the catalyst for a series of measures that reinforced the mechanism of terror. On 9 September a Parisian revolutionary army was set up, consisting of 7200 sans-culottes under the command of a former soldier and radical activist, Charles-Philippe Ronsin. Its function was to patrol the departments around the capital in search of food and political suspects [101]. Price controls were placed on grain and fodder on 11 September, and on 29 September a 'general maximum' enforced general wage and price controls: wages were pegged at 50 per cent above their 1790 level, and food and basic necessities at 33 per cent above. All rates were to be set locally by district authorities, and in mid-October the Committee of Public Safety set up a Central Food Commission headed by one of its own members, Robert Lindet, to supervise food distribution and the application of the maximum [1]. To reinforce the political terror, the law of suspects, passed by the Convention on 17 September, expanded the revolutionary tribunal to four separate courts, with two functioning at any one time, and authorised revolutionary committees throughout the country to arrest 'political suspects'. These 'suspects' were broadly defined to include royalists, federalists, any administrator dismissed from office since 1789, former nobles who lacked a consistent record of loyalty to the revolution, and anyone who criticised the revolution in any way. The impact of the law was immediate: the prison population of Paris trebled over the next three months, from 1417 to 4525, and the revolutionary tribunal which had ordered the guillotining of just 66 prisoners between mid-March and mid-September guillotined 177 between late September and the end of the year [124]. Several prominent political figures were among them, including Marie-Antoinette (16 October), the leading Girondin deputies (31 October), and Madame Roland, wife of the Girondin minister of the interior Jean-Marie Roland (8 November).

[iii] Terror in the provinces

The most dramatic increase in the terror came in the provinces in the wake of the defeat of the federalist and Vendéan revolts. The Vendéan army was convincingly defeated for the first time at Cholet on 15–17 October, and some 80 000 of its bedraggled members – including priests, women, and children – headed north to the Channel port of Granville in the hope of receiving reinforcements and supplies from the British navy. They failed to capture the town, and were forced back southwards towards the Loire in disarray, to be defeated at Le Mans on 13–14 December. Most of the survivors were then massacred at Savenay nine days later in what the commander of the republican armies, Westermann, called 'horrible butchery'. Yet the butchery still had a long way to run, for in its decree of 19 March 1793 the Convention had already authorised military courts to execute rebels summarily within 24 hours of their capture (see chapter 3). Some 4354 were shot from the late autumn onwards in Laval on the orders of the Vokler military commission, and a further 1123 in Angers, where at least 1020 more died of disease in prison before they could come to trial. In Nantes, over 3000 prisoners died in overcrowded prisons, and a further 2100 were executed on the orders of the Lenoir and Bignon commissions during the winter of 1793–4, under the vigilant eye of the representative on mission, Jean-Baptiste Carrier. The Bignon commission alone ordered over 1900 executions in three weeks between 29 December 1793 and 19 January 1794, with most of its victims shot by firing squad in nearby quarries, and buried in anonymous mass graves by the local civilian population. The *noyades* made even this process look humane, for by mid-November, with prisoners dying daily from disease in overcrowded prisons, members of the local revolutionary army – the 'Marat Company' – sought Carrier's approval to short circuit the judicial procedures. Carrier agreed, and the Marat Company herded prisoners on to barges at night, under cover of darkness, then floated the barges out into the river Loire where they were holed, leaving their victims to drown [97, 101]. There are no accurate records of the numbers of *noyades* or their victims, but best estimates suggest that there were between six and eleven between mid-November and the end of January, with a total death toll of between 1800 and 4860 [96].

Meanwhile, the federalist revolt had come to an end too. Marseille had surrendered on 25 August after a short siege, Lyon and Bordeaux capitulated in October, and Toulon finally capitulated on 19 December [161, 111, 118, 104]. There too victory opened the way for retribution. After Toulon's surrender on 19 December over 700 ringleaders of the revolt were shot without trial within a week, and a military commission then sentenced a further 283 to death [104]. The figures would certainly have been higher if several thousand rebels had not escaped with the British fleet in the last days of the revolt. In Marseille the two representatives on mission in charge of the repression, Barras and Fréron, set up a revolutionary criminal court which sent 289 people to the guillotine between August 1793 and the following spring, and its work was supplemented by a military commission which executed a further 123 [161]. In Lyon the death toll was much larger, for it was a city dominated by wealthy silk merchants who had shown little enthusiasm for the revolution, and had been the centre of counter-revolutionary conspiracies since 1789. Its leading role in federalism merely convinced Parisian Jacobins that wealth and counter-revolution went hand in hand, and both the Convention and the Committee of Public Safety were therefore determined to punish the guilty, and intimidate any potential support for resistance elsewhere. As soon as the siege ended the Convention changed the city's name to 'Liberated Town', ordered the houses of the rich to be destroyed and decided that a column was to be erected in the middle of the ruins with the inscription: 'Lyon waged war on liberty: Lyon is no more' [154]. The representative on mission in charge of the final stages of the siege was Georges Auguste Couthon, a member of the Committee of Public Safety; but he declined to enforce repression on the scale that the Committee wanted, and was replaced by one of his more radical colleagues, Collot d'Herbois. Collot was accompanied by Joseph Fouché from the Committee of General Security, and together the two men set up a revolutionary commission which sentenced 1673 people to death between late November and the following April. A further 213 victims were executed on the orders of the departmental criminal court, bringing the total death toll to over 1800 [143]. Most of the victims were guillotined or shot, but in early December Collot and Fouché decided to accelerate the process by ordering the army to carry out mass executions by cannon fire, on the Brotteaux plain on the edge of the city. Sixty prisoners were killed in so-called *mitraillades* on 4 December, and 211 on the following day. The carnage was appalling. Dozens of victims were wounded rather than killed, and had to be finished off by hand. The troops complained, the officers protested, and the experiment was quickly abandoned in favour of a return to more traditional methods. The firing squads and the guillotine continued their work for another four months [144].

Incidents such as the *mitraillades* and the *noyades* were not simply the work of anarchic or sadistic representatives on mission who were running out of control, for the Committee of Public Safety was kept informed of what was going on, and raised no objection at all. Quite the contrary, it regarded the victims of the *noyades* as outlaws who had betrayed the revolution, and the victims of the *mitraillades* as convicted traitors. Both groups had therefore put themselves outside the bounds of 'civilised' society [111, 144]. Yet barbaric executions were the exceptions rather than the rule, for the vast majority of deaths were ordered by legally established revolutionary courts which applied the Convention's legislation. Moreover, the repression of federalism was not uniform, for in the chaotic conditions of late 1793 representatives on mission enjoyed a great deal of freedom in the way that they used their powers. In Normandy, where the federalist revolt centred on Caen had collapsed in July, Robert Lindet used a conciliatory approach: only two administrators directly involved in the revolt were executed, while the rest received short prison sentences or were simply acquitted. In Bordeaux, Claude-Alexandre Ysabeau was keen to ingratiate himself with the city's merchant elite, and Jean-Lambert Tallien fell under the influence of a mistress, Thérèse Cabarrus, who used her physical charms to protect local families. So, although both men promised the Committee of Public Safety that they would show 'indulgence towards the poor' and 'severity towards the educated rich', the military court that they set up to punish federalist leaders executed only 104 people during the winter of 1793–4 [118]. In Alsace, where one of the 'hawks' on the Committee of Public Safety, Saint-Just, was involved in reinforcing the army of the Rhine during November and December in a province well known for its opposition to the revolution, he achieved his objectives without a single execution [130].

[iv] The reinforcement of the Committee of Public Safety

Saint-Just's activity in Alsace formed part of the other success story of the Committee of Public Safety in late 1793 – its achievements against the First Coalition. A British attempt to capture Dunkirk was defeated at Hondschoote on 6 September while a large Austrian army was defeated at Wattignies on 16 October, leaving French armies in almost total control of north-eastern France. In Alsace, Saint-Just tackled a combined Austrian and Prussian invasion with the help of two newly promoted generals, Hoche and Pichegru, and by the end of the year the invasion forces had been all but driven out [49, 130]. Success strengthened the reputation of the Committee of Public Safety, and quickly led to an extension of its powers. On 10 October the Convention decreed that government would remain 'revolutionary until the peace', and put the Committee in charge of ministers, generals, and other government committees. Two months later the law of 14 Frimaire (4 December 1793) confirmed it as the major power in central government by defining its powers more precisely, and streamlining its chain of command. Departmental administrations were stripped of most of their political powers, and district and municipal administrations were upgraded to become responsible for the enforcement of revolutionary legislation. To ensure central government control of their work, national agents were to be appointed to them by the Committee of Public Safety, with the duty of providing regular reports to Paris on their work. Additional provisions of the law reined in the autonomy of representatives on mission, who were now required to report to the Committee every ten days, and to restrict their activities to those permitted by law. All revolutionary armies other than the Parisian army, which had been authorised in September, were also disbanded. In effect, the Committee now controlled the levers of power at central and local government level, and France had effective centralised government for the first time since 1789 [14, 154].

In the short space of six months the republic had lurched from political purge to revolutionary dictatorship which used terror to silence its opponents. The death toll had risen dramatically as a result, from a handful of executions in the early summer to over 3000 in the month of December [124]. Civil war played a major role in this escalation. The ferocity of repression in the Vendée was prompted by a genuine belief that the revolt there was an integral part of an international conspiracy to restore the ancien régime. That was a tragic misreading of the real origins of the revolt, which was rooted in deeply felt popular resentment against the revolution's religious, administrative, and taxation reforms. Yet it was not a misreading of the revolt's effect, for it forced the republic to divert military re-sources away from the war front when invasion was under way, and provided a welcome toehold for British intervention and assistance. Neither was Jacobin violence against the rebels a one-sided affair, for from its outset the revolt had been marked by the kind of savagery on both sides that civil wars frequently display. Fouché's and Collot's severity in Lyon, along with the executions in Toulon, Marseille, and elsewhere in the Midi, were similarly prompted by the belief that federalism was part of an international conspiracy. This too was mistaken, for federalists were moderate republicans whose major 'crime' lay in opposition to Jacobin radicalism, yet it was the inevita-ble result of the political intolerance that had been a growing feature of both revolutionary and counter-revolutionary ideology since 1789.

Sans-culotte pressure played an important part in this escalation of the terror by forcing the Convention to strengthen the revolutionary tribunal, extend the definition of political suspects, and impose economic controls which were enforced by the anarchic activities of the revolutionary armies. Yet the Convention itself was not just a passive force, for deputies themselves came to regard terror as a legitimate political weapon, as federalism, political assassination, and the Vendée finally convinced them that moderation and conciliation were counter-productive. By the end of 1793, Jacobins had come to regard all opposition to the revolution as the product of royalism, and themselves as responsible for navigating the revolution through a dark sea of political conspiracy and treason. Even friends or allies could quickly change shape into royalist agents, and only a firm response could break the vicious cycle of defeat, and ensure that the republic survived. In his speech to the Convention introducing the 10 October decree, Saint-Just had mapped out the survival path for the revolution, which reflected a new and draconian approach to all forms of opposition: 'You have no longer have any reason for restraint against enemies of the new order.... You must punish not only traitors but the apathetic as well; you must punish whoever is passive in the Republic.... We must rule by iron those who cannot be ruled by justice' [130: 132–3]. So far the 'iron' of the guillotine and the gun had been used only on rebels, but soon it would be used against mere critics as the terror began to take an ominous turn.

5 Factions Liquidated: December 1793–April 1794

It was to take several weeks and months for the Frimaire law to take full effect, as communication problems meant that it took time for the text itself to percolate down to the more remote provincial towns and villages. Even when it arrived, some revolutionary armies continued to operate well into the early months of 1794, and several representatives on mission continued to ignore the letter of the law, resenting the way in which their colleagues in Paris were reducing their independence and freedom of action [138]. The task of enforcement was painful and slow, but just as it seemed that the Committee of Public Safety was winning, a dispute erupted in Paris over future policy which threatened its position. A group known as the Indulgents argued that military success provided the opportunity for the terror to be safely scaled down, and for normal constitutional government to return. A rival group, the Hébertistes, argued instead that military success was only a start and that terror now needed to be intensified in order to root out counter-revolution for ever. The argument began in December 1793 and raged into the spring of 1794, dividing the Jacobin club and threatening the Committee's authority until it finally intervened by despatching both groups to the guillotine. By doing that it changed the terror from a weapon against civil war to a mechanism for enforcing political uniformity.

[i] The Committee of Public Safety and the Hébertistes

Despite the increased powers given it by the Frimaire law, the Committee of Public Safety remained a sub-committee of the Convention, and its membership was formally renewed by deputies every month. In practice, from September onwards its success ensured that its membership remained stable until the summer of 1794, with the sole exception of Hérault de Séchelles, who was guillotined in the spring of 1794 because of his involvement with political extremism.

Of its members, Maximilien Robespierre is the best known, for although he occupied no specific leadership role on the Committee, he was frequently its spokesman in the Convention and the Jacobin club on questions of policy and principle. A lawyer from Arras in north-eastern France, he had been elected to the Estates-General in 1789, and rapidly forged a reputation for himself as a democrat and an 'incorruptible' man of integrity. The nickname of 'Incorruptible' stuck, and Robespierre was not afraid to be unpopular, as he showed in his dogged opposition to the Girondin war policy during the winter of 1791–2 [169]. Yet he also developed a deeply suspicious attitude towards all political colleagues and a tendency to see any view other than his own as the result of plots and conspiracies against the public good. Elected to the Committee in late July 1793, he was influential in formulating policy in conceptual terms which used Rousseau's ideas on virtue and the general will. Behind the rhetoric he was also an intensely political animal who worked hard to keep the divergent opinions within the Committee of Public Safety together during the winter of 1793–4 [128]. Close to him was Louis Antoine de Saint-Just, a deputy from the department of the Aisne, who was just 26 years of age, and had risen to prominence during the king's trial a year previously, with his implacable insistence on the need for a political execution [130]. Lazare Carnot, a former army officer, master minded military strategy with the assistance of Prieur de la Côte d'Or, Prieur de la Marne, and Jeanbon Saint-André. Robert Lindet and Georges Couthon proved to be efficient administrators, and Bertrand Barère used the oratorical skills of his legal training to present the Committee's policies to the Convention [120]. Billaud-Varenne and Collot d'Herbois had been added to the Committee on 6 September to boost its radical credentials. Billaud was a lawyer with a radical past in the Paris sections and Jacobin club, while Collot was an actor before his election to the Convention in 1792 [99, 142].

All the Committee's members, except for Hérault, came from solidly middle-class backgrounds, but their political experience and temperaments were widely divergent. Some, like Robespierre and Saint-Just, were idealists who came to see terror as a chance to transform France into a utopian democracy based on patriotism and civic virtue. Others, such as Carnot and Lindet – neither of whom ever joined the Paris Jacobin club – were pragmatic patriots who saw it primarily as a way of winning the war. The secret of their cooperation lay in the fact that the republic's survival, in the winter of 1793–4, was a more pressing concern than its ultimate shape. As a result these 11 very different men worked together effectively, some spending long hours on mission in the provinces while others stayed in the Green Room of the Tuileries Palace, which acted as their political and administrative base. Correspondence with deputies on mission in the provinces or with government agents took up much of their time, but so too did military planning, policy decisions, and the drafting of legislation. It was a relentless daily routine which included participation in Convention debates or Jacobin club meetings, and which frequently stretched from early morning until late at night.

[ii] The Hébertiste challenge

Despite its hard work and its military success, the Committee of Public Safety faced a growing political challenge in the latter months of 1793, led by the popular radical journalist Jacques René Hébert. Hébert had been an influential political figure since the summer as his newspaper, the *Père Duchesne*, had given him a national audience which stretched far beyond his sans-culotte readership in Paris. Although not a member of the Convention, he was a member of the Cordeliers and Jacobin clubs, and of the Paris Commune. He also had political allies in the radical hotbed of the Ministry of War, where the minister's secretary, François Vincent, systematically recruited sans-culottes militants into positions of influence. In ideological terms, Hébert was something of an opportunist who had moved to the left during the summer of 1793 to neutralise the Enragés by supporting sans-culotte demands for economic controls and more terror. His influence had grown with the sans-culotte invasion of the Convention on 5 September, which produced the general maximum and the law of suspects. The Committee of Public Safety and the Convention had tried to clip the sans-culottes' wings during the following weeks by arresting the Enragé leaders, Jacques Roux and Jean-François Varlet. In late October it also ordered the closure of the Society of Republican and Revolutionary Women, which was closely linked to the Enragés [87, 133, 160]. The meetings of the Paris sections were reduced to two per week in early September, and poorer sans-culottes provided with a small payment for attendance, in the hope that their presence would dilute the influence of militants at meetings. Yet neither measure had much effect, as most sections merely established popular societies to meet on the other five nights of the week, in which militants continued to play a powerful role [166].

Indeed, during October, Hébert's influence was increased by the spread of de-Christianisation. Relations between the revolution and Christianity had been steadily deteriorating since the split caused by the civil constitution of the clergy in 1791. By the summer of 1793 even juror priests were viewed with suspicion because of the failure of the constitutional church to attract popular support. As a result Christianity itself came under attack. The first step towards a complete break came in early October, when the Convention voted to introduce a new revolutionary calendar that dated time not from the supposed birth of Jesus Christ, but from the foundation of the French republic in September 1792. The period from 22 September 1792 to 21 September 1793 now became Year I, the corresponding period from September 1793 to September 1794 was Year II, and so on. The months were renamed after the seasons, so that the month from 22 September to 21 October was named Vendémiaire (harvest time), the following month Brumaire (mist), November to December became Frimaire (frost), and so on. Each of the new months contained 30 days, which were divided into three ten-day weeks, or *décades*, with a rest day on every *décadi* or tenth day. Those left over at the end of each year were called *sans-culottides* [9].

The purpose behind the calendar was as much political as religious, reflecting the Convention's determination to mark its break with a royalist and Christian past. Yet the change came at a time when physical attacks on Christianity were beginning in the provinces. In late September Joseph Fouché, representative on mission in the department of the Nièvre, inaugurated a bust of the Roman hero Brutus in the cathedral of Saint-Cyr in Nevers. Three days later he condemned clerical celibacy, and ordered priests in the diocese to adopt a child or an old person as proof of their commitment to the republic. Then, on 10 October, he ordered the replacement of Christianity throughout the department by a new cult of the republic, ordering cemeteries to be secularised and the words 'Death is eternal sleep' posted at their gates [95].

Fouché's actions were matched by other representatives on mission. In the departments of the Somme and the Oise, André Dumont closed down churches and forced priests to resign, while in the cathedral at Reims, Philippe Ruhl solemnly broke the flask of conse-crated oil used for royal coronations [88]. Their motives were mixed. Many, such as Fouché, had been members of religious orders prior to 1789, and now saw de-Christianisation as a way of purging their past and proving their commitment to the secular ideals of the revolution. Others were more interested in using anticlericalism to rally the support of local militants against moderate administrators who were clinging on to power, while some were swept along on a tidal wave of popular anticlericalism among local sans-culottes, who identified Christianity with superstition, social control, and counter-revolution [71, 141].

Whatever the reasons for the sudden explosion, de-Christianisation reached Paris in early November, and Hébert became one of its most enthusiastic supporters. On 6 November the Convention closed down all Parisian churches, and on the following day the city's archbishop, Jean-Baptiste Gobel, appeared before the Convention flanked by several of his priests to announce that he was abandoning the priest-hood. Over 400 priests in the diocese followed suit, and the Paris Commune promptly organised a Festival of Liberty on 10 November in the cathedral of Notre Dame, which was renamed the Temple of Reason for the occasion. A 'mountain' was built inside the cathedral, with a 'Temple of Philosophy' perched on top, from which a 'Goddess of Liberty' – who was in fact a well known Parisian singer – emerged at the appropriate moment [134]. Similar ceremonies were organised in provincial towns, and by the end of the year most churches throughout the country had been transformed into temples of reason, or converted into food stores, prisons, and saltpetre factories. Some 20 000 priests (out of a pre-revolutionary total of 130 000) abandoned the priesthood, and 6000 of them married as proof of their definitive commitment to the secular life [171].

Despite the popular enthusiasm with which sans-culottes greeted de-Christianisation, the Committee of Public Safety was opposed to it because of its potential effect on the peasantry who, for the most part, remained deeply religious. Robespierre in particular suspected the twin driving forces behind it to be atheism and counter-revolution, both of which he believed to be using the movement for their own ends. Although no longer a Christian in any meaningful sense, he was a deist who shared the Enlightenment belief in a 'supreme being' responsible for creating the universe and still benignly watching over human affairs. Most of the leading activists in de-Christianisation were closer to atheism in their beliefs, and Robespierre regarded that as a recipe for immorality and social chaos. He disliked the political aspects of the movement too, because many of its supporters were foreigners who mixed in the same circles as Hébert: men such as Pierre Proly, the illegitimate son of the Austrian foreign minister, Jacob Pereyra, a Jewish merchant of Portuguese origins, and Anacharsis Cloots, the son of a Dutch merchant who had been involved in radical politics and the spread of the revolution abroad since 1790.

Along with many of his colleagues on the Committee of Public Safety, Robespierre suspected many of these of being secret enemy agents, and he had some reason for doing so. In mid-October, a deputy in the National Convention, Fabre d'Eglantine, had warned the Committee of General Security that several of his fellow deputies were involved in financial and political corruption. A large state trading company, the East India Company, had been liquidated by the Convention during the autumn, and several deputies, according to Fabre, had been bribed to forge the liquidation decree in order to ensure that the shareholders received windfall profits. In mid-November another deputy, François Chabot, went to Robespierre with similar allegations, adding the suggestion that several of the radicals and foreigners who supported Hébert on issues such as de-Christianisation were being paid by foreign governments to destabilise and discredit the revolution [129]. According to Chabot, corruption and radicalism were twin components of a 'foreign plot', master minded by the British prime minister, William Pitt, through a Parisian agent, the Baron de Batz. Chabot was probably inventing much of this in order to divert attention from his own involvement in the financial corruption of the East India affair, but there was enough of a murky underworld at work in Paris for the Committee of Public Safety to believe his story and suspect Hébert of treason. As a result, on 6 December Robespierre halted de-Christianisation in its tracks by persuading the Convention to confirm the principle of religious freedom in a decree that prohibited any further church closures [71, 128].

[iii] The Indulgent campaign

The decree had a minimal impact on church closures but it did have an effect on the political situation. For Robespierre and the

Committee of Public Safety were supported in their stand against de-Christianisation by Danton and a group of deputies known as the Indulgents. Danton had been removed from the Committee of Public Safety in early July, yet he remained an influential figure at the Jacobin club, and among his allies there was a fellow deputy, Camille Desmoulins [127]. Desmoulins launched a newspaper in early December 1793, the *Vieux Cordelier*, to campaign for an end to the terror, choosing his title deliberately to evoke the spirit of the Cordelier club as it had existed during the early period of the revolution, before it had been taken over by Hébert's supporters. In his first two numbers he defended Danton and criticised Hébert, and in the third number he condemned de-Christianisation, and called for a scaling down of the terror [90]. The *Vieux Cordelier* was an instant success. The early print runs sold out rapidly, and Desmoulins' criticism of extremism and terror became the main talking point in cafés and political clubs. On 17 December the Convention reflected the changing mood by ordering the arrest of François Vincent, secretary to the minister of war, and Charles-Philippe Ronsin, commander of the Paris revolutionary army, both of whom were prominent Hébertistes. Three days later it set up a clemency committee to review the cases of all political prisoners and release the innocent.

Until this stage Robespierre appears to have supported the Indulgent campaign. He was a personal friend of Desmoulins, had read the proofs of the *Vieux Cordelier* before it went to press, and seems to have approved of their content. However, just when it seemed that the terror was about to be scaled down, two events intervened to halt the Indulgent momentum. The first was the return to Paris of Collot d'Herbois on 21 December to answer criticism of the severity of his handling of the federalist revolt in Lyon [143]. Speaking in the Jacobin club immediately on his return, Collot attacked critics of the terror, and defended the guillotine as a vital weapon in the fight against counter-revolution. This alarmed Robespierre, who feared that the Committee of Public Safety might be split by the issue, and he quickly went back on his initial support for Desmoulins. In the *Report on the Principles of Revolutionary Government* to the Jacobin club on 25 December he attacked both moderates and extremists as enemies of the revolution, and he went on to defend the terror as a necessity of war. The revolution, he argued, was the 'war of liberty against its enemies,' and terror was essential to its success. On the following day the Convention disbanded the clemency committee that it had voted to establish just a few days previously, and all hopes of an early end to the guillotine's work faded.

The second event to put the Indulgents on to the defensive was the discovery by the Committee of General Security in early January that Fabre d'Eglantine, who had denounced the forging of the East India Company decree to them in mid-October, had himself been involved in the forgery. It concluded that Fabre had denounced others in order to cover up his own guilt, and promptly ordered his arrest on 13 January 1794. The discovery raised the possibility that moderates had been campaigning for clemency only in order to conceal their own corruption, and convinced the Committee of Public Safety that they were in fact working secretly with extremists in a plot to destabilise the revolutionary government and sabotage the revolution. In a speech to the Jacobin club on 8 January 1794, Robespierre denounced 'a new political faction' with two heads: moderates who called for an end to the terror and radicals who wanted it intensified. Both, according to Robespierre, were out to wreck the revolution.

[iv] The elimination of Indulgents and Hébertistes

Lacking concrete proof of its suspicions, the Committee played for time while police investigations into Fabre's case continued. However, the investigations dragged on, and in early February Vincent and Ronsin, who had been imprisoned in December as a result of the Indulgent campaign, were released from prison because the Committee of General Security could find no evidence to support the allegations against them. They were determined to gain their revenge, and quickly denounced the Indulgents who had helped put them there, and the Committee of Public Safety that had supported them. By early March they were openly calling for an insurrection to 'save' the revolution from its moderate enemies, and Hébert supported them in his *Père Duchesne* by denouncing the 'sleepwalkers' on the Committee of Public Safety. The Hébertiste challenge came at a difficult time for the Committee, as food shortages in Paris were reviving sans-culotte militancy, and workers in the building trade and munitions factories were calling for higher wages [78]. Political radicalism and economic crisis had proved dangerous on several occasions before, so the Committee acted swiftly to pre-empt trouble. On the evening of 13 March Saint-Just warned the Convention that the

Hébertiste campaign was part of a foreign plot against the revolution, and next evening the leading Hébertistes were arrested and sent before the revolutionary tribunal on a charge of plotting to starve Paris, establish a military dictatorship, and betray the revolution to its enemies. The charges were clearly fictitious, but the revolutionary tribunal did its duty by finding all but one of the defendants guilty. They were guillotined on 24 March.

With Hébert gone, the Committee purged prominent radicals from the Paris sections, and disbanded the Paris revolutionary army, which had been a stronghold of Hébertisme since the previous September. The popular societies that had acted as alternative centres for political debate in the sections since that September were bullied into closing their doors, and 38 of them disbanded during the next two months [150]. The Cordeliers club lost all its political influence, and Hébert's allies on the Paris Commune were replaced by men loyal to the Committee of Public Safety. The purge even extended to the provinces, where Hébertistes were removed from several departmental and municipal administrations, and purged from popular societies and Jacobin clubs [109]. Yet their elimination left the Committee open to pressure from the Indulgents, whom it was convinced were equally dangerous. On 18 March 1794 it therefore decided to send Fabre d'Eglantine to the revolutionary tribunal, on charges of corruption and treason, along with several other politicians involved in the East India Company affair. However, most members of the Committee knew that Danton was almost certain to oppose the trial, because of his friendship with Fabre, and wanted him arrested too. Robespierre hesitated because of his long friendship with Danton, since the early days of the revolution, and in late March had two secret meetings with him in an attempt to persuade him to remain silent. But Danton refused, so on the night of 30–31 March he too was arrested, along with Camille Desmoulins. The trial was a stormy one, and Danton defended himself so vigorously that he was removed from the courtroom on the second day. That made the verdict inevitable, and on 5 April he and his colleagues were found guilty, and guillotined that same evening. Eight days later the widows of Desmoulins and Hébert followed their husbands to the guillotine, both convicted of treason, despite the fact that they had married into opposing political factions [127].

The execution of the Hébertistes and Dantonists was not the first political purge of the revolution. The guillotining of royalists after the fall of the monarchy in August 1792 has the best claim on this dubious honour, followed by the execution of the king five months later, and the Girondins at the end of October 1793. The revolution had by now become accustomed to executing defeated politicians and liquidating political factions, in the belief that all were involved in a giant web of counter-revolutionary intrigue which embraced both the Vendée revolt and federalism. There is little doubt that, by the spring of 1794, members of both governing committees sincerely believed that Hébert and Danton were counter-revolutionaries, even though they lacked the evidence to prove it. In that sense, both factions were the victims of political trials which used fabricated evidence to 'prove' counter-revolutionary involvement and, as the trial of the Girondins had shown in late October, lack of evidence was no obstacle to a guilty verdict from the revolutionary tribunal. What was new about the so-called 'purge of the factions' in the spring of 1794, however, was the fact that it was an act of political cannibalism exercised by Jacobins upon themselves. The terror was beginning to devour its own as the governing committees used the guillotine to exterminate not just opponents of Jacobinism but rival factions within it. The lessons of that were ominous, for both Hébert and Danton had been political giants, and if men of their stature could be wiped out by the revolutionary tribunal, nobody was safe. Their deaths therefore marked a very real watershed, for political debate from now was liable to be a dangerous affair if it offended the governing committees. The Indulgent campaign for an end to the terror, and the Hébertiste call for its radicalisation, had therefore not just failed. Instead, both had achieved the opposite of their intentions by giving the revolutionary government a reason for denouncing all criticism as counter-revolutionary conspiracy. Once it was able to do that, it was free to develop terror into a weapon of political orthodoxy that would prove infinitely more frightening than anything the ancien régime had ever dreamed of.

6 The Guillotine and Regeneration: April–July 1794

The spring and summer of 1794 were to prove the most controversial phase of the revolution because of the combination of an escalating execution rate with sweeping social and moral reform. The intensification of terror at a time when the threat posed by war was receding has always proved difficult to explain. By the spring of 1794 there were no foreign armies left on French soil, no rebellion threatening to undermine central government, and no open political opposition to the Committee of Public Safety's authority. What happened was therefore not the result of 'circumstance', in the normally accepted sense of a defensive response to invasion or civil war, but the result of a deliberate political decision to crush dissent and mould French society into a new and utopian form. Quite clearly, the Committee of Public Safety saw itself as still surrounded by enemies, but the definition of those enemies was constantly expanding, and it responded with yet more centralisation, more terror, and more reform. It was a simple but brutal recipe which produced the 'great terror' of June and July 1794, during which more people were guillotined in Paris in six weeks than had been decapitated during the whole of the previous 15 months. The guillotine, strategically placed in the Place de la Révolution (now the Place de la Concorde), now became the symbol of the revolution.

[i] Centralisation and the Prairial law

With Hébert and Danton disposed of, the Committee of Public Safety was firmly in control of political life. Convention debates developed into a monotonous endorsement of its policies and a servile celebration of its achievements, while all but one of its presidents during the summer of 1794 – the equivalent of a modern parliamentary speaker – was a member of either the Committee of Public Safety or its sister committee, the Committee of General Security. The Committee of Public Safety tightened its grip on power in other ways too. On 1 April the six ministers were replaced by 12 executive commissions, whose members were appointed by itself. This eliminated the possibility of ministries developing into rival power bases, as the Ministry of War had done during the previous year when Bouchotte had made it a centre of sans-culotte militancy. On 16 April, it was also authorised to supervise administrative personnel throughout the country, and within days it set up its own police bureau with specially recruited informers and the power to carry out arrests [140].

Secure in its control of central government, the Committee also reinforced the machinery of political repression. On 18 April the Convention ordered the transfer of all political prisoners in the provinces to Paris, to stand trial before the revolutionary tribunal instead of departmental courts. Three weeks later, on 8 May, all provincial commissions and revolutionary courts were closed down, and the revolutionary tribunal in Paris was given a virtual monopoly over political justice. That monopoly was made more effective when, in late May, assassination attempts were made on Collot d'Herbois and Robespierre. They were both rather bizarre affairs. In the first, a rather solitary individual, Henri Admirat, waited around outside Robespierre's lodgings and, when he did not turn up, tried to shoot Collot d'Herbois instead. He failed because the pistol jammed, but the following day a young girl, Cécile Renault, turned up at Robespierre's lodgings and insisted on seeing him. Her manner aroused suspicion, and when she was arrested she was found to be carrying a small dagger. The two incidents were the work of individuals acting alone, but they aroused fears of a counter-revolutionary plot to assassinate members of the Committee of Public Safety, and the response was the law of 22 Prairial (10 June 1794), which radically streamlined the procedures of the revolutionary tribunal. According to its provisions, the accused now lost the right to a lawyer (article 16), and could be convicted on the basis of moral rather than material proof (article 9), while jurors could use their conscience in coming to their verdict when the evidence was insufficient. Article 6 of the decree also extended the definition of political crimes to include anyone who criticised patriotism, 'persecuted' patriots, or attempted to 'deprave morality'. Any attempt to 'dilute the energy and purity of revolutionary principles' was declared an offence, as were plots against the security and survival of the republic. For the guilty, the only punishment was death, while the acquitted were allowed to go free; imprisonment was no longer an option [112].

Historians have been almost unanimous in their condemnation of the Prairial law. Aulard, for example, the republican historian of the late nineteenth century, condemned it as 'a butchery of the innocent and guilty alike, worthy of the rule of kings or of the Inquisition; a slaughter which cannot be excused on the grounds of national defence, as by that time France was safe' [2: *vol. 2, 287*]. Yet most of them have interpreted it in different ways. For convinced socialists such as Albert Mathiez early in the twentieth century, the Prairial law was a weapon in Robespierre's programme for the redistribution of wealth, by accelerating the execution of counter-revolutionaries. For Georges Lefebvre, also a socialist but more guarded in his assessment of Robespierre, it was primarily a response to the assassination attempts made by Admirat and Renault, and to military problems on the north-eastern frontier. Yet neither explanation is entirely convincing. Most recent research suggests that Robespierre had no long-term plans for wealth redistribution, while the provisions of the Prairial law bear too many resemblances to legislation that had gone before to be viewed merely as a reflex response of fear. Instead, it seems probable that, while the timing of the law may have been affected by Admirat's shots and Renault's dagger, its content built on the previous development of the terror and was part of its ultimate logic: all criticism and all social or political deviation were suspect by definition, and legal niceties were a hindrance rather than a help to the implementation of true 'revolutionary' justice. It is best interpreted, therefore, as a further tightening of the ratchet of political and moral regeneration.

Whatever its explanation, the Prairial law transformed the revolutionary tribunal into a high-speed conveyor belt to the guillotine. The lack of a defence lawyer and of the need for evidence, coupled with the extension of political 'crimes' to almost any human activity, put most of the population at risk of eventual arrest and execution. By July 1794, over 7500 prisoners were crammed into overcrowded Parisian jails, and their processing by the revolutionary tribunal was being made easier by the use of *fournées* (batch trials), in which dozens of prisoners who hardly even knew each other were lumped together under the same general charge of treason. The first *fournée*, which involved 73 prisoners, took place on 16 June, and another eight of them followed during the next four weeks. In the 15 months between March 1793 and the Prairial law, the revolutionary tribunal had sentenced 1251 prisoners to the guillotine at an average rate of just under three per day; between mid-June and the end of July it was to send 1376, at a rate of over 30 per day [124].

Despite the centralisation of revolutionary justice in Paris, some executions continued in the provinces too, in areas where the Committee of Public Safety allowed exceptions to the Germinal law on centralisation. In Nîmes, the departmental criminal court executed 33 people for their support for federalism during the previous summer, while in Bordeaux the Committee of Public Safety's agent, Marc-Antoine Jullien, revived a military commission set up after the federalist revolt in the previous October, and guillotined 198 prisoners during June and July [67, 118]. In the Vaucluse, a military commission executed 332 victims on charges of federalism and counter-revolution, while in the north-east a military commission in Arras and Cambrai executed a further 492 [108, 135]. Meanwhile, in the Vendée, the killing process dispensed with courts altogether, for after the defeat of the rebellion in December the Committee of Public Safety had ordered the commander of the army of the west, General Louis-Marie Turreau, to eliminate all remaining rebels. Turreau split his troops into two armies of 12 columns each, which then converged on the Vendée from east and west with orders to kill men, women, and children who had taken part in the revolt, and to burn farms, villages, and woods. The work of Turreau's 'infernal columns' began in late January and ended in mid-May, leaving thousands of civilians dead, and hundreds of acres of farmland devastated [145].

The summer months of 1794 therefore saw the death toll, which had begun to decline in the early spring, rise again. Never again was it to reach the giddy levels of the winter months, when repression in Lyon and the Vendée had carried the monthly average of executions to over 3000, but by July the average had nonetheless risen to over 1400 and, in stark contrast to the winter months, most of the executions were taking place in Paris. Small wonder, then, that the sight of mass executions sickened public opinion to the extent that the guillotine was relocated in the Place de la Nation, on the outskirts of the city. In addition to the resurgence in numbers, the social profile of the terror was also beginning to change [124]. During the terror as a whole, between March 1793 and July 1794, approximately 7 per cent of the terror's victims were priests, 8 per cent nobles, 25 per cent middle class, 28 per cent peasants, and 31 per cent artisans or labouring poor (the latter two percentages reflecting high peasant and artisan involvement in the revolt in the Vendée). These figures suggest that the nobility and clergy were certainly guillotined in greater proportion than their percentage of the overall population, but this was more because of their higher participation in opposition to the revolution than because of their social class itself. The figures changed, however, during the 'great terror' of June and July as the proportion of nobles rose to 20 per cent, priests to 12 per cent, and the upper middle class to 26 per cent. During these two months nobility, clergy, and upper middle class made up almost 60 per cent of the guillotine's victims, suggesting that the terror was now targeting not just those actively involved in counter-revolution, but the 'undesirable' social categories of the rich and religious who were passively identified with it, and who by their very status were judged incompatible with a revolutionary republic. The terror, in other words, was developing into a social war [124, 146].

[ii] Social and moral regeneration

This change in emphasis was reflected in the priority given to social and moral regeneration by the Committee of Public Safety [126, 152]. Since 1789 the revolution had set out to build a new social and political order in France, based on the foundations laid by Enlightenment ideas. Initially, many had hoped that the change would come quickly and spontaneously as the institutions of the ancien régime were swept away and man's natural goodness allowed to flourish in a revolutionary environment. But as the revolution ran into difficulties, it was accepted that the whole process would be slower, requiring a lengthy period of political education. Robespierre, for example, noted in the autumn of 1792 that: 'To draft our political institutions we should need the morality that the institutions themselves must eventually produce' [126: 56]. Eighteen months later, in the spring of 1794, his colleague on the Committee of Public Safety, Saint-Just, echoed his pessimism, noting that: 'A revolution has taken place within the government but it has not yet penetrated civil society' [126: 58].

The Committee's policies of social and moral regeneration were a logical result of this belief that moral change had to be encouraged by the government. As Billaud-Varenne said in a speech to the

Convention in April 1794: 'To put it bluntly, we must re-create the people that we wish to make free, for we need to destroy old prejudices, change outdated customs, restore jaded feelings, restrain excessive wants and annihilate deep rooted vices' [99: *162*]. On the social side, most Jacobins subscribed to the Enlightenment view of man as naturally good, and believed that individual freedom would lead to a harmonious and prosperous society. As a result, they believed in a free market economy, except in periods of war or crisis, when price controls and economic regulation by the state were temporary necessities. They also supported the principle of private property, in the belief that property gave people the independence and dignity that they needed to lead virtuous and useful lives, but combined this with a suspicion of wealth and of the temptations that it brought with it. In this they were influenced by Rousseau's belief that virtue was more often found among the simple poor than among the sophisticated rich. Their social ideal, as a result, was that of the pre-industrial small and independent producer – self-sufficient peasants, artisans, shopkeepers, and the wage-earning labourer – with the role of government defined as promoting civic virtue rather than social revolution, and as helping the poor to gain access to property.

The Convention had already been edging towards social reform with the general maximum of 29 September 1793 which pegged food prices within the reach of the urban poor for much of Year II and propped up the value of the paper currency, or *assignat*, in which most wage earners and artisans were paid. A law of 10 June 1793 had also begun to tackle the land hunger of the rural poor, by allowing villages to divide up common land equally between all their inhabitants if a third of the community requested it. On 17 July all remaining vestiges of feudalism were finally abolished, and in September it was decided to give landless rural families a voucher guaranteeing a 20-year interest-free loan to buy church or émigré land. Before the end of the year the Convention decided to sell off that land in small parcels to bring it within reach of the poor, and on 6 January 1794 the inheritance laws were changed so that all children gained an equal share of the family property on their parents' death [64].

In the spring of 1794, the Committee of Public Safety pushed the process further by deciding to redistribute the property of political criminals to the poor. On 26 February and 3 March, Saint-Just presented to the Convention the Ventôse decrees (named after the current month in the revolutionary calendar), which stated that the deserving poor were to receive property confiscated from 'enemies of the people'. Six commissions were to review the cases of political suspects, while municipalities throughout the country were ordered to draw up lists of the deserving poor in their area. The poor would then be given property confiscated from convicted suspects, whose punishment would thereby solve the problem of poverty. Introducing the decrees, Saint-Just argued that they represented the dawn of a social revolution, and socialist historians, writing in the late nineteenth and early twentieth centuries, took him at face value, interpreting the decrees as an early attempt at a socialist redistribution of land from the rich to the poor [148]. If this had really been the case, it would have been only a drop in the ocean, for the property of political suspects would have done little to dent the very real poverty experienced by many millions of the urban and rural poor. Quite what they would have done with a small plot of land allocated to them in a lonely rural commune several hundred kilometres away is also open to doubt. Modern scholarship, however, suggests that Saint-Just's intentions were probably more limited. Both he and his colleagues on the Committee of Public Safety wanted to increase the punishment for counter-revolution, and offer some hope of consolation to the Parisian sans-culottes at a time of acute food shortages. Many of them probably also saw it as a way of calming sans-culotte discontent at a time when the Committee was planning the arrest of Hébert and his Cordelier colleagues. Certainly there was no rush to implement the legislation, and only two of the six commissions had been set up by the time that the Committee fell from power in the autumn of 1794 [166].

More progress was made in direct poverty relief, for since the confiscation of church property in 1789, religious charity, which had been the mainstay of poor relief prior to 1789, had all but collapsed. Successive attempts to replace it with a secular alternative had failed because of lack of money and adequate organisation, but on 19 March 1793 the Convention decreed the establishment, in principle, of a national system of public welfare. Three months later, on 28 June, it ordered the founding of a national maternity hospital and a hostel in each district, to provide for the needs of unmarried mothers and abandoned children. The law of 11 May 1794 (22 Floréal II), however, set up a comprehensive welfare scheme for the poor in rural areas, ordering the opening of a Great Book of National Charity in each department, in which the names of the elderly in need, the ill, and of widows or deserted mothers with children were to be listed. The number eligible for assistance was fixed for each department, in proportion to its population, and annual sums fixed for each category. Poor or ill peasants over the age of 60, who had 20 years of work behind them, were to receive 120–160 livres per year; artisans over 60 who had worked 25 years were to get the same, while deserted mothers with three or more children – or widows with two – were to receive 60 livres. The amounts involved were small, but they were intended as a basic supplement and the scheme was moderately successful in many of the rural departments where poverty was widespread [117].

The Committee of Public Safety's major problem in all its attempts to tackle social reform was its lack of money, and this was also a problem in the area of moral reform. The right to education, for example, had been included in the Declaration of Rights of the abortive 1793 constitution, and in July 1793 the Convention approved a somewhat spartan scheme, drawn up by the deputy Michel Lepelletier, who had been assassinated six months previously, for the creation of 20 000 state boarding schools to provide compulsory education for boys from the ages of five to 12. Away from their parents for seven years, they were to receive a strict egalitarian education, all wearing the same clothes and receiving identical lessons, that was designed to mould them into loyal citizens. The scheme was never implemented because of money problems and, instead, on 19 December 1793 (29 Frimaire II) the Bouquier law provided for all boys to receive three years of free, compulsory, and secular primary education. They were to learn reading, writing, and arithmetic, as well as receiving instruction in the principles of the Declaration of the Rights of Man. Municipalities would license teachers and supervise schools, but the state would pay their salary and provide official textbooks [155]. Bold on paper, the scheme proved a failure in practice because of lack of money, and a survey in October 1794 found that less than 10 per cent of districts had opened their full quota of schools [134].

A more sustained effort was put into civic education for adults. Control of the printed word was central to this, and the law of suspects was used to close down newspapers, and guillotine their editors and printers. By the summer of 1794 the only newspapers that survived were those that repeated the mantras of Jacobin orthodoxy, and some were subsidised by the Committee of Public Safety, which also ran its own newspaper, the *Feuille de Salut Public*. Other forms of propaganda were encouraged too. The *Recueil des Actions Héroiques et Civiques* was a periodical with a print run of 150 000 that featured the heroic deeds of soldiers and civilians in defence of the republic [134]. On the stage, a decree of 2 August 1793 ordered the closure of any theatre which ran plays sympathetic to royalty, and subsidies were provided for new plays which promoted republican virtues. Some 500 of them were staged between the summer of 1793 and the autumn of 1794, most of them celebrating military victories or condemning the alleged vices of the ancien régime [159]. Poets were called upon to celebrate the achievements of the revolution, and the fine arts were also mobilised through the efforts of Jacques-Louis David, a member of the Committee of General Security. The finest French painter in the neo-classical style, David produced several portraits of revolutionary martyrs, including the assassination of Marat [107].

One of the most powerful propaganda weapons at the government's disposal was the network of political clubs, or 'popular societies', affiliated to the Jacobin club in Paris. In the summer of 1793, when the terror began, there were just over 3000; by the summer of 1794, the number had doubled to over 6000, with a heavy concentration in Normandy, the frontier departments of the northeast, and Provence. In the countryside, popular societies were often small affairs, with memberships of less than 100, but in towns and cities their memberships frequently ran into several hundred [94]. Local politicians were usually members, and the main order of business revolved around newspaper readings, correspondence from other clubs, and political debates. Government agents, representatives on mission, and army generals usually made them their first point of call, and clubs usually worked with the local revolutionary committees in ordering the arrest of political suspects and purges of local administrations [149].

One final area of revolutionary propaganda was religion. Since de-Christianisation in late 1793, Christian worship had collapsed in most parts of the country. Thousands of priests had married, while others had abandoned the priesthood or gone into hiding or exile [171]. Yet most members of the Committee of Public Safety and the Convention remained deists, convinced of the existence of a supreme being, and of the necessity of religious belief for social order and morality. This was particularly true of Robespierre, who had opposed de-Christianisation at the end of 1793 because of its associations with atheism, and

62

who remained determined to restore some kind of religious worship to the new Jacobin republic. In a report to the Convention on behalf of the Committee of Public Safety on 7 May 1794, Robespierre proposed the creation of an official cult dedicated to the supreme being. Its central feature was to be a national programme of festivals, organised within the structure of the revolutionary calendar, and designed to encourage virtue. There were to be public acts of worship every tenth day (*décadi*) commemorating significant events and republican virtues, such as the 'love of the fatherland', 'benefactors of humanity', world freedom, modesty, stoicism, love, childhood, old age, and happiness. The Convention endorsed the plan and a month later, on 8 June, the inaugural Festival of the Supreme Being was held in Paris. As president of the Convention at the time, Robespierre presided over the event, which was meticulously organised by David, the painter and member of the Committee of General Security. A huge and carefully organised procession made its way initially to the Tuileries Palace, where Robespierre delivered a speech in praise of the supreme being and condemning atheism, before a papier maché model of atheism was solemnly burnt. The procession then went on to the Champ de Mars, where a huge artificial mountain had been built to symbolise the Jacobin 'Mountain' in the Convention. Music played, songs of praise to the supreme being were sung, incense burned and, as a mark of respect, the guillotine's work was suspended for the day [151].

[iii] Conclusion

The republican historian, Aulard, argued that the Cult of the Supreme Being, like so much of the terror, was basically a political tactic designed to rally public opinion behind the war effort in the weeks that preceded the crucial summer campaign. Albert Mathiez, a fervent supporter of Robespierre and lifelong critic of Aulard, argued instead that it was Robespierre's way of building on the positive aspects of de-Christianisation, by creating a patriotic religion, shorn of the superstitious aspects of Catholicism, which would be capable of attracting Catholic support and providing a moral basis for the regime. Political or spiritual? The Cult of the Supreme Being probably contained elements of both, for although Robespierre and his colleagues were well aware of the political advantage of restoring some form of religious worship – particularly attractive to the peasantry, who had never approved of de-Christianisation – they also ensured that the values of the new religion were closely linked to their Jacobin ideals, and to the kind of social utopia that they wanted to create by the end of the war.

In that way the supreme being and the guillotine formed part and parcel of the same project of regeneration and extermination that had lain at the heart of the great terror since the spring. Both were designed to bring the revolution to an 'end' by ensuring military victory in war and the moral regeneration of the French people. To modern eyes, appalled by the catastrophe of totalitarianism and social engineering in Stalin's Russia, Mao's China, and Hitler's Germany, it is a chilling prospect built on a frightening agenda. Why then did it happen? Fatigue and fear no doubt played some part, for the Committee of Public Safety was by now made up of tired men who had been working under pressure for several months, and their frayed nerves had difficulty coping with criticism or opposition. It should not be forgotten either that not all plots and opposition were the figment of their imagination. Many plots had undoubtedly existed since 1789, and there is little doubt that Pitt and the British did have agents working in Paris during the spring of 1794. The circumstance argument cannot be entirely ruled out of play either, for although the Vendée was by now under control and foreign armies had retreated from French soil since late 1793, the military situation remained finely balanced until the stunning successes of French armies that were yet to come in late June and July. Defeat may not have been staring the revolution in the face in the early summer of 1794, but the reflections of previous defeats were still flashing in the political mirror. Yet that mirror was also increasingly filled with Jacobin ideology, under the influence of Rousseau; the Jacobins had become convinced that they alone were able to judge the 'general will' that ought to be at the heart of a truly democratic society. Spurred on by their belief that the general will should govern the interests of society, many members of the Committee of Public Safety had become convinced that their own opinions were the general will, and justified to themselves the extermination of all opposition. Attracted by the hope that revolutionary government provided the means to reshape society in such a way that a new and egalitarian France could emerge by the end of the war, they used all the powers of a centralised state to regenerate France's moral and social structures. In the end, the corruption of power lured them towards attractive but unattainable goals, but within weeks the realities of power were to bring the whole experiment to a bloody end.

7 Terror as Failure: The Return of Normality, 1794–5

What would have happened if the terror had gone on beyond the summer of 1794 is difficult to predict. It is doubtful that the land distribution mapped out in the Ventôse legislation or the annual payments provided for in the charity decrees of May would have made significant inroads into the problem of poverty, because the scale of the problem was too large. The Cult of Supreme Being would never have developed into a national religious cult because it was too political and too abstract for rural France, while educational reform needed a great deal more time and money to make its impact felt. Yet there is every reason to believe that the guillotine had a long life ahead of it, for almost 8000 prisoners were locked up in Parisian jails by July 1794, and the figure was rising daily. At the current execution rate of 30 a day, it would have had to continue its work for at least another year to empty the cells and, even when it had finished, the transition from dictatorship to democracy would have been traumatic. As a subsequent French leader, Charles de Gaulle, once noted, dictatorships in France usually end in a messy way.

[i] The growth of disillusion

In the event, the mess came before the terror was over, for although war pressure had encouraged political centralisation, military victory took away that justification and the Committee of Public Safety became the victim of its own success. In the spring of 1794 French armies began to move forwards on a number of fronts, using the huge troop numbers generated by the mass levy decree of the previous autumn and the expertise of a new generation of freshly promoted young generals. Carnot coordinated strategy on the Committee of Public Safety, as French armies invaded Sardinia in April, and crossed the Pyrenees into Catalonia during May. Yet it was in the north-east that the main effort was concentrated, with the four armies of the north, the centre, the Ardennes, and the Moselle concentrating their offensive on Austrian positions. On 18 May the Austrians were defeated at the Battle of Tourcoing, and five weeks later, on 26 June, Jourdan inflicted a decisive defeat on them at the battle of Fleurus. Within two weeks he had gone on to Brussels, and by the end of September France was in control of the whole of Belgium. The war was far from over, but defeat was now a remote possibility and politicians could safely quarrel [49].

The decline of the sans-culottes made political quarrels safer too. Even at the height of their power, in the summer and autumn of 1793, sans-culotte activists had made up only around 10 per cent of the total male population. By the summer of 1794 that number had dwindled significantly because of general disillusion [166]. Despite the general maximum, food supplies remained scarce in Paris during the spring, and although the Committee of Public Safety relaxed its provisions in February, to allow a greater margin to peasants and encourage more produce to come on to the market, they allowed no rise in wage rates to compensate for higher prices. During the spring of 1794 a wave of strikes broke out in the state-controlled armaments factories and printing works and, to add insult to injury, the Paris Commune produced a wage schedule for Paris on 23 July which applied the regulations of the general maximum rigidly, and slashed the existing wage rates by up to a half [78]. Political apathy reinforced the effects of economic discontent, for the execution of Hébert during the spring had stunned most sans-culottes, causing many of them to lose interest in a political process that they could no longer influence or control. By the summer months most sections had fallen into the hands of small cliques of professional revolutionaries, paid by the government for their work on section committees, and operating as passive cogs in the government machine [98, 102]. The sans-culotte movement no longer posed a threat to the Convention or to the Committee, but the dynamism that had made it such a powerful ally of Jacobinism over the previous year had been fatally sapped. Little wonder that, when Robespierre was later taken to the guillotine, sans-culottes who had idolised him the year before lined the streets, shouting 'Fuck the maximum!' [1].

Support for the terror was dwindling in the Convention too. Most deputies had only ever supported it as a way of dealing with military defeat and civil war, and now wanted the killing to stop and normal parliamentary government to return. Their own necks counted for something in this mood swing, for many had been friends of Danton and bitterly resented his execution. They feared that the finger of suspicion might soon be pointed at them, and were joined in this by several representatives on mission who had been recalled to Paris by the Committee during the spring and summer months because of their extremism or because they were suspected of corruption. In a general atmosphere of fear, all were aware that the Committee's spies were watching their every move. Although none of them dared to criticise the Committee openly, many of them discussed the possibility of action secretly, and were waiting for the right moment to move [140].

[ii] The fall of Robespierre

That moment eventually came because of mounting conflict between the Committee of Public Safety and the Committee of General Security over a number of issues. The Committee of Public Safety's police bureau, set up in April to monitor the activities of administrative personnel, had the power to carry out arrests, which cut across the police functions of the Committee of General Security, causing some resentment. The potential for friction increased with the introduction of the law of 22 Prairial (10 June), which was drafted by Robespierre and Couthon for the Committee of Public Safety without reference to their colleagues, or to the Committee of General Security, which had responsibility for police matters [113, 137]. Religion widened the rift, for several members of the Committee of General Security were atheists, who detested the Cult of the Supreme Being. Within days of the inaugural festival of 8 June they showed their disapproval by ordering the arrest of a 78-year-old religious mystic, Cathérine Théot, who claimed to be the 'Mother of God' and held mystical seances in her apartment in central Paris which were attended by known counter-revolutionaries. During the seances she apparently read passages from the Bible which predicted the arrival of a new messiah, and when Marc Vadier, of the Committee of General Security, reported on her arrest to the Convention on 15 June, he made several sarcastic references to religion. These were clearly aimed at Robespierre, who had played a prominent role in the festival of the supreme being, and although Robespierre hit back by having her trial deferred, the bitterness in Vadier's attack was plain for all to see [112, 114].

Yet Robespierre was also at the centre of growing divisions within the Committee of Public Safety, where the pressure of work was beginning to take its toll, and personality conflicts which had stayed beneath the surface for much of the previous ten months began to emerge. Saint-Just disagreed with Carnot over military tactics for the spring offensive [128], Collot d'Herbois never forgave Robespierre for criticising the severity of his work in Lyon, while both Collot and Billaud-Varenne resented the way in which Robespierre and Couthon had drafted the Prairial law without consulting them. Most of the tensions revolved around Robespierre, for although he had been an excellent Committee member for much of the year, sensitive to the feelings of his colleagues and anxious to preserve government unity, by the summer of 1794 he had become difficult and distrustful. Distrusting all forms of criticism, he was increasingly convinced that he was surrounded by conspirators who were intent on destroying the achievements of the previous year. In late June he had a violent quarrel with Billaud-Varenne, Collot, and Carnot, and for the next three weeks stopped attending meetings of the Committee of Public Safety altogether. Instead, he worked on government papers in his lodgings with the Duplay family, and confined his political discussions and speeches to the Jacobin club [128]. It was political suicide, but for some months he had been talking of the possibility of his own martyrdom in the cause of the revolution, and may have even welcomed the prospect as a way of proving his own devotion to the cause of virtue [92].

Once the rift became public knowledge it threatened government unity, and a joint meeting of the two committees was held on 22 July to patch up a compromise. Robespierre was invited to attend a meeting on the next day, which he did, and he appeared to endorse the agreement. Yet three days later, on 26 July, he launched a bitter attack on his colleagues in the Convention. Claiming that yet another plot to destroy the republic was being organised, he called for a purge of both the Committee of Public Safety and the Committee of General Security, but failed to name the people he wanted arrested or to define the policy changes that were necessary [140]. Stunned by the attack, the Convention deferred a decision. This gave Robespierre a chance to repeat his charges to the Jacobin club that evening, but it also gave his colleagues on the two governing committees time to organise their retaliation. When the Convention met next day, 27 July, or 9 Thermidor Year II in the republican calendar, Robespierre was arrested along with his brother, Augustin, and two colleagues from the Committee of Public Safety, Couthon and Saint-Just. One of his allies on the Committee of General Security, Philippe Lebas, was arrested too. The Paris Commune promptly defied the Convention and released all five men, transporting them to the town hall, the Hotel de Ville, and calling on units of the National Guard to support their stand. But it was a hopeless cause, for the bulk of the sans-culottes had lost confidence in Robespierre since Hébert's death, and only a few battalions turned out. Most of them drifted home shortly after midnight after standing around for hours in the rain waiting for orders that never came, and the Convention then sent in National Guards from the wealthier western sections of Paris to bring the resistance to an end. By three in the morning it was all over. Lebas killed himself with a single shot to the head. Augustin Robespierre jumped from a top floor window and broke his thigh on the street below. Couthon, who had been paralysed from the waist down since childhood, threw himself from his wheelchair down a stone stairway and lay concussed at the bottom with a head injury. Robespierre tried to shoot himself, but succeeded only in blowing away most of his lower jaw, while Saint-Just just waited stoically for his capture and inevitable fate [91]. On the evening of 28 July, at seven o'clock, all four survivors were executed as outlaws, without trial, along with 18 of their supporters. During the next two days some 83 members of the Paris Commune were decapitated too in the three bloodiest days of the terror.

[iii] The end of the terror

The power struggle on 27–28 July had little to do with ending the terror, for that had never been Robespierre's intention, and there is even less evidence to suggest that his opponents on the two committees wanted it. Speaking in the Convention on 29 July, Barère claimed that the revolutionary government had emerged from the crisis stronger than ever, and the Committee of General Security showed its intentions of carrying on business as usual by issuing a torrent of arrest warrants against Robespierre's supporters. Yet it had badly misjudged the political situation, for the terror collapsed within weeks as the Convention seized its chance to reassert its political authority. On 29 July it decided that a quarter of the membership of all committees would be replaced every month, so destroying the continuity of personnel that had been a key element in the Committee of Public Safety's hold on power for almost a year. The three vacant places left by Robespierre, Saint-Just and Couthon were promptly filled by moderates, and by the end of August only three members of the old Committee remained in place. On 24 August its powers were cut back to cover just war and diplomacy, while responsibility for domestic policy was distributed among 15 other committees. The Prairial law was repealed on 1 August, and the prosecutor of the revolutionary tribunal, Fouquier-Tinville, was arrested. Shortly afterwards the tribunal's procedures were changed, restoring the defendant's right to a lawyer and to call witnesses, and all the judges and jurors were replaced. The execution rate dropped dramatically, and prisons began to empty as friends and relatives clamoured for the release of prisoners. By the end of August over 2000 prisoners had been set free, and a wave of releases had begun in the provinces too. Nine months later, on 31 May 1795, the revolutionary tribunal was abolished altogether [177].

As the terror collapsed, the political backlash began [175]. Press censorship was dismantled as dozens of pamphlets and newspapers poured on to the streets, denouncing the terror and calling for revenge. Fréron and Tallien, who had been representatives on mission in Marseille and Bordeaux enforcing the terror just nine months earlier, now encouraged the formation of armed youth groups, the *jeunesse dorée*, who assaulted prominent Jacobins and sans-culotte activists. In early November the *jeunesse* forced the Paris Jacobin club to close down, and most of the provincial clubs closed their doors in the months that followed. In December Jean-Baptiste Carrier, who had been representative on mission in Nantes at the time of the *noyades*, was sent before the revolutionary tribunal and guillotined for his role in encouraging them, and before the end of the year the Convention set up a committee to investigate the activity of former members of the Committees of Public Safety and General Security during the terror [97]. On 2 March three of them – Barère, Billaud-Varenne, and Collot d'Herbois – were put under house arrest and later sentenced to deportation to Guyana. In May Fouquier-Tinville was guillotined for his work as public prosecutor.

Political reaction and personal vengeance soon spread to the provinces as a 'white terror', so called after the colour of the flag of the Bourbons, erupted in the Midi. It was particularly virulent in areas involved in the federalist revolt during the summer of 1793, where the Jacobin terror had been most brutal. During the winter of 1794–5 secret royalist groups, calling themselves the Company of Jesus or the Company of the Sun, began carrying out revenge attacks on Jacobins [69, 102]. The first mass murder happened in Nîmes in late February 1795, when several Jacobin administrators were lynched by the National Guards who were escorting them to prison, but the pace quickened after a law of 10 April 1795 which ordered the disarming of all known Jacobin activists. Over 100 Jacobins were murdered in prison massacres in Lyon on 4 May; 60 more followed in Aix-en-Provence a week later, and over 100 in Marseille in early June. By the end of 1795 some 2000 Jacobins had been murdered in the south-east alone, with little or no effort on the part of local administrations or central government to bring the killing to a halt [139, 178].

The fate of the Jacobins was shared by the Parisian sans-culottes [182]. Their political power had been already been curtailed by the Committee of Public Safety during the spring of 1794, but the screw was now tightened further. Section meetings were reduced from two to one every ten days, the powers of the revolutionary committees which had ordered the arrests of suspects were drastically cut back, and the middle class began to reassert their political influence in section meetings. The sans-culottes were also hit by economic changes, as the Convention abandoned price controls and abolished the general maximum on 24 December 1794, in the mistaken belief that a return to the free market would solve food shortages and lower prices. Yet the winter of 1794–5 proved to be the harshest of the century. Rivers froze over, transport was virtually paralysed, and food supplies ran low. The crisis was made worse by a collapse in the value of the *assignat*, which drifted down to 7.5 per cent of its face value by the following May. The cost of living doubled in the first four months of 1795, and starvation, hypothermia, and suicide became common among the poor, while the rich could survive by paying the high prices demanded on the open market. Deprivation on this scale had the effect of reviving sans-culotte radicalism in the form of two sans-culotte uprisings, on 1 April 1795 and 20 May. Crowds from the poorer eastern sections of the capital invaded the Convention on both occasions, calling for bread and the implementation of the long forgotten 1793 constitution. Just two years previously a sans-culotte invasion of the Convention had forced the arrest of the Girondins and launched the terror; but times had now changed. Jacobin deputies now formed only a tiny minority, and deputies were better prepared. Both insurrections were crushed, Jacobin deputies who had supported them were executed by a military commission, and over 1200 sans-culottes arrested. Several thousand were also disarmed, and there was to be no sizeable popular revolt in Paris again until 1830 [176].

With the sans-culottes under control, the Convention abandoned the radical 1793 constitution and drafted a more moderate replacement, the constitution of Year III, which established the regime known as the Directory. Its work done, it met for the last time in late October 1795 after over three years of continuous work. Yet the Directory failed to provide a stable political regime. Its legislature was divided between two houses: the Council of Five Hundred and the Council of Elders, its franchise was carefully manipulated to ensure that deputies would be drawn from the well off propertied classes, and the five directors who made up the executive were not allowed to sit in the legislature. The whole structure was designed to create a middle way between monarchy and Jacobinism, but the middle way proved difficult to find in a country badly divided by social and political conflict since 1789, and still at war. There was no return to the terror, although several deputies were arrested and deported after a coup d'état in the autumn of 1797. Yet the regime was never stable and finally collapsed in late 1799 as a military coup d'état brought the young Corsican general Napoleon Bonaparte to power. Five years later the republic which had been proclaimed in 1792 was abandoned altogether as Napoleon crowned himself emperor in an elaborate ceremony in the cathedral of Notre Dame.

Conclusion

History has moved on since 1789, but many of the issues raised by the French revolution remain relevant to twentieth-century France. A broad view of the revolutionary and Napoleonic period between 1789 and 1815 would suggest that it contains three basic political models: constitutional monarchy (1789–92), democratic republic (1792–1804), and Napoleonic Empire (1804–15). French politics since 1815 have largely recycled these three categories, with two attempts at constitutional monarchy between 1815 and 1848, a repeat version of the Napoleonic Empire between 1852 and 1870, and a succession of republics in 1848–52 and from 1870 onwards.

When François Furet launched the revisionist approach to the revolution in 1978, he argued that, with the collapse of French communism and the decline of the traditional right, France had at last escaped from its revolutionary legacy. The events of 1789–94 could now be examined dispassionately, without the need to make constant comparisons between the revolutionary experience and contemporary political conflict. 'The Revolution,' he argued, 'is over' [27: *11*]. Yet preparations for the bicentenary celebrations during the 1980s showed that both revolution and terror remained very much live issues. The political context of the decade played an important part in this, for the dramatic collapse of communist regimes in central and eastern Europe revived controversy over the legitimacy of revolution as a tool of social and political change. Marxist and Jacobin historians had often compared the achievements of Lenin with those of Robespierre, as both men had led revolutionary governments based on an alliance between a radical middle-class elite and a popular movement [36]. Lenin himself had often compared the Bolshevik revolution of 1917 with the terror of 1793–4 [42]. Yet in the 1980s the comparisons concentrated more on the negative impact of revolutionary dictatorship. For many critics of communism, the fall of the Bastille was being paralleled 200 years later by the collapse of the Berlin wall, and the totalitarian ideology of Russian communism was under attack. The revolution was clearly not 'over', and although Furet himself has always rejected the use of his ideas to suggest that the terror was a precursor of modern totalitarianism, other historians were less reticent [27, 41].

Historians are never fully detached from the world in which they live, yet the danger with reading the past too closely from the perspective of the present is that it too often forces events into a predetermined shape. All sides in the debate over the terror – conservatives, revisionists, and circumstance historians alike – have been guilty of this, with the result that none of them has an entirely convincing case. Yet that does not mean that all are equally valid, for this book has argued that the conservative interpretation of the terror, which condemns it as the key principle underlying the revolution from 1789 onwards, lacks the evidence to make its arguments stick. Stronger on political polemic than on historical research, it can safely be discounted. The revisionist interpretation, on the other hand, makes a much stronger case. It overstates the role of ideology and the influence of Rousseau. In its anxiety to move away from the social history approach of Marxist historians, it also downplays the role played by social conflict, and underestimates the importance of counter-revolution in escalating the atmosphere of political violence. By claiming that the political agenda of the revolution was predetermined by the ideology of 1789 it presumes that ideology was the all-powerful motive force behind events, and defines that revolutionary ideology in an unacceptably narrow way. In a curious way it uses ideological determinism in the same way that the Marxist historians which it denounces use economic determinism to explain human behaviour. As a result it completely overlooks the way in which the revolution evolved between 1789 and 1794, how certain political options were taken and others ignored, and how events influenced decisions. On the other hand, by exploring the ambiguities of Jacobin ideology on popular sovereignty, probing the links between the absolutism of the ancien régime and revolutionary intolerance, and stressing the significance of Jacobin ambitions for moral and political regeneration, it has focused attention on the role of ideas in diverting the revolution from the path of constitutional politics and into the political practice of terror.

For its part, the circumstance argument needs to be handled with care too. At its most basic, as argued by Mignet and Thiers in the early nineteenth century or by Aulard towards the end, it is plainly too simplistic. To portray terror as simply a patriotic response to the threats of counter-revolution and war is to ignore the disparity between challenge and response in areas such as the Vendée, and to leave unexplained the escalation of the rate of execution in the summer of 1794, when the worst of the threat had clearly passed. War and counter-revolution were probably important in causing the terror, but as subsequent wars in France have not produced similar terrors, political context is clearly as important as the crisis itself [154].

A balanced explanation of the terror has to explain the way in which events and ideology came together to create a unique mentality in 1793–4, and this can be done only by placing both in the context of the development of the revolution. The initial reforms of 1789 to 1791, as we saw in chapter 2, were designed to combine constitutional government with popular sovereignty and individual freedom. But the lack of a parliamentary tradition, and of a sufficiently broad consensus on reform, created a conflict between left and right, patriot and counter-revolutionary, which poisoned the political atmosphere. This might not have led to terror, as we saw in chapter 3, had the Girondins not raised the political stakes by launching an aggressive and expansionary war in the spring of 1792. The economic and military pressures that war generated created the need for political centralisation, and encouraged a tactical alliance between radical Jacobins and Parisian sans-culottes which formed the political spring-board for the terror. In an atmosphere of crisis, Girondins and Jacobins accused each other of treason and, once counter-revolution and federalism erupted in the spring of 1793, that language of suspicion precipitated the slide towards terror. What began as a political purge of the Girondins developed into a generalised system of repression, as successive 'factions' were eliminated and guillotined. Finally, the Prairial law in the summer of 1794 transformed the vast majority of French people into potential political suspects.

Circumstances played a central part in this degeneration, for without war the crisis would never have been as serious, without the Vendée and federalism the fear of treason would have been less pervasive, and without the political wrangles within Jacobinism the acute suspicion of political dissent might never have developed to the degree that it did. Yet if the crisis had not hit a political culture in which intolerance had built up over four years, and in which a Jacobin minority sincerely believed that the regeneration of the human race was at stake, terror would not have been the end result.

If the terror was the result of several factors, what of its consequences? Death was the most obvious, and the guillotine its most powerful image. The best analysis of the death toll of the terror, written over 60 years ago by the American historian Donald Greer, puts the figure of official executions between March 1793 and the end of August 1794 at 16 594 [124]. This covers executions in both Paris and the provinces, but a further 40 000 were executed without trial (in the Vendée or in federalist cities such as Toulon) or died in prison awaiting trial. To them must be added at least 200 000 deaths from civil war in the Vendée, bringing the total figure to a minimum of 260 000 [145]. There may well have been several thousand more. Yet death was neither indiscriminate nor universal. The numbers of executions were highest in areas of civil war and federalism: 3548 (21 per cent of the national total) took place in the single department of the Loire-Inférieure, where Carrier was active in Nantes in the winter of 1793–4. In the wider area of the Vendée there were 8674 executions (52 per cent of the total), and a further 3158 (19 per cent) occurred in the south-east, in the wake of the federalist revolts in Lyon, Marseille, and Toulon. Another 910 (6 per cent) died in federalist departments of the south and south-west as well, bringing the total for federalism and counter-revolution to 77 per cent. The other departments with high execution rates lay in frontier areas invaded by Austrian, Prussian or British forces: 551 people (3.5 per cent) were executed in three departments on the north-eastern frontier, and a further 243 (1.5 per cent) in the east. If we add to all these departmental figures the 2639 victims executed in Paris (16 per cent), then 98 per cent of all executions are covered. Several departments that were far removed from military invasions or federalist activity saw no deaths at all, and a further 34 departments – mostly in the centre of the country or in mountainous areas such as the Alps – witnessed less than ten. The overwhelming majority of victims therefore came from areas of war and counter-revolution, and died for their opposition – or supposed opposition – to the authority of the Convention. This is well illustrated by analysis of the crimes that they were charged with, for no less than 93 per cent were executed for emigration, sedition, treason, conspiracy, or royalism. A mere 1.5 per cent died for 'economic' crimes such as hoarding or ignoring the general maximum. In Greer's words:

'it would be difficult to ignore the inference that the Terror was an instrument of political repression used principally against the bitterest enemies of the republic' [124]. Further proof of this comes from the monthly rhythm of deaths, for after a slow start in the summer of 1793, when the monthly rate was rarely more than 100, there was a sharp rise from September onwards which peaked with a total of 3517 in January 1794, when the repression in Lyon and Nantes was at its height. It then dropped during the spring of 1794, before rising again to over 1000 per month in June and July, as a result of the Prairial legislation.

If we turn from the death toll of the terror to its political impact, its main achievement was probably to save the revolution from disintegration and defeat. Yet that 'achievement' was by no means a clear-cut case of cause and effect, for repressive Jacobin policies often aggravated the problems that they were directed against, and transformed that problem into a crisis. More sensitivity in handling the Vendée's grievance, for example, might have avoided a major civil war in the spring of 1793. Similarly, in the federalist revolt, a recent study of Lyon has argued that Jacobin arrogance was counter-productive, spoiling the very real chance that existed during the early stages of the revolt for a negotiated settlement [111]. To some extent the terror was therefore a self-generating event, creating through its own intransigence increased opposition which then 'justified' more violence. Yet this argument can only be taken so far, for the politicians of the Convention were forced to work at speed during 1793, under intense pressure, and deprived of the advantages of hindsight that historians enjoy. The problems facing them in the spring of 1793 called out for centralised government and effective measures against both civil war and foreign invasion. This the terror achieved, although in doing so it discredited many of the ideals on which the revolution had originally been based.

Two important political traditions also emerged from the terror. The first was republican democracy, based on universal male suffrage, parliamentary democracy, and the separation of church and state. This tradition resurfaced briefly during the Second Republic of 1848–52, and then more durably in the Third, Fourth, and Fifth Republics from 1870 onwards. The second was social democracy, which drew its inspiration from the social reforms of the Committee of Public Safety, and looked on the state as the agency for social reform and the alleviation of poverty [181]. This was something which an early French socialist, Gracchus Babeuf, was to attempt to resurrect in 1795–6, in his unsuccessful 'Conspiracy of Equals', which aimed at establishing a revolutionary dictatorship for the carrying out of a social revolution [178, 181]. It then reappeared in socialist thought of the 1830s and 1840s, during the July Monarchy, and has remained an important feature of it ever since. On a less ideological level, the terror also had an administrative impact on France by strengthening the structures of the state. Over a century ago Alexis de Tocqueville pointed to the paradox that the revolution created a more centralised form of government than the absolutism that it replaced [16]. It initially abolished royal *intendants* in favour of an elective form of decentralised government, but drifted back towards centralisation by the summer of 1793 because of political division and war requirements. The Frimaire law in December 1793 anchored this drift, and although the Directory repealed the law, administrative centralisation remained in place under a different guise. Napoleon merely consolidated the practice with the creation of prefects and, until the reforms of the first Mitterrand presidency in the 1980s, France remained one of the most centralised countries in Europe. If the revolution marked the beginning of 200 years of political instability, the terror therefore bequeathed a tradition of administrative centralisation which enabled politicians to disagree without endangering the survival of the state. That in itself was no mean achievement, but whether it was one that Robespierre and his colleagues would have recognised as worthwhile is another matter.

Chronology

This date list is confined to major events and is intended to help readers establish the basic chronology of the terror. It does not include every incident mentioned in the text.

1789

5 May	Opening of the Estates-General in Versailles
17 June	Third Estate adopts the title of 'National Assembly'
14 July	The fall of the Bastille
4–11 August	The National Assembly decrees the 'abolition' of feudalism
26 August	Declaration of the Rights of Man and of the Citizen is completed
10 September	Assembly decides on a bicameral legislature for the new constitution
11 September	King is provided with a suspensive veto
5–6 October	Demonstrators march from Paris to Versailles, forcing the royal family to move to Paris

1790

19 February	Execution of the Marquis de Favras for counter-revolutionary conspiracy
May–June	Counter-revolutionary riots in Montauban and Nîmes
12 July	The civil constitution of the clergy is passed
27 November	All priests ordered to take an oath to the constitution

1791

January–March	Oath to the civil constitution splits priests into jurors and non–jurors

20 June	Flight to Varennes
17 July	'Massacre' of the Champ de Mars
13 September	Louis XVI accepts the constitution
1 October	Legislative Assembly meets
9 November	Law orders the émigrés to return within two months (vetoed)
29 November	Assembly asks the king to order the electors of Trier and Mainz to remove the émigrés from his territory

1792

10–23 March	King appoints a Girondin ministry under Dumouriez
20 April	France declares war on Austria
13 June	Girondin ministers dismissed
20 June	Sans-culottes invade the Tuileries Palace
10 August	Insurrection forces removal of the king; Legislative Assembly orders elections for a National Convention
2–7 September	The 'September massacres' in Paris
20 September	Battle of Valmy
21–22 September	National Convention meets and declares France a republic
19 November	First propaganda decree promises help and fraternity to oppressed peoples
10 December	King's trial begins
15 December	Second propaganda decree states that French armies will dismantle the ancien régime in conquered areas

1793

14–17 January	Convention condemns the king to death
21 January	Louis XVI executed
1 February	France declares war on Britain and Holland
24 February	Levy of 300 000 recruits ordered for the army
10 March	Decrees send representatives on mission to the provinces and establish the revolutionary tribunal in Paris
10 March	Beginnings of revolt in the Vendée

19 March	Convention decrees that armed rebels to be executed within 24 hours of capture
21 March	Surveillance committees (*comités de surveillance*) established
6 April	Convention creates the Committee of Public Safety
15 April	Paris sections ask the Convention to expel Girondins
4 May	Price controls imposed on grain
29 May	Moderates oust the Jacobin municipality in Lyon
2 June	Leading Girondins purged from the Convention
24 June	Convention passes the 1793 constitution
10 July	Danton and moderates removed from the Committee of Public Safety
13 July	Charlotte Corday assassinates Marat
26 July	The Convention votes for the death penalty for hoarders
27 July	Robespierre voted on to Committee of Public Safety
1 August	Convention orders a scorched earth policy in the Vendée
9 August	Public granaries to be established in every district
23 August	The *levée en masse* decree
29 August	Toulon surrenders to the British fleet
5 September	Sans-culottes invade the Convention
6 September	Collot d'Herbois and Billaud-Varenne added to Committee of Public Safety
6–8 September	British and Dutch defeated at Hondschoote
9 September	Convention decrees the setting up of the Paris 'revolutionary army'
17 September	Law of suspects
29 September	Convention passes general maximum
5 October	Convention adopts revolutionary calendar
10 October	Convention declares government of France 'revolutionary until the peace'
12 October	Fabre d'Eglantine denounces a 'foreign plot' to the Committee of General Security
16 October	Austrian army defeated at Wattignies
16 October	Execution of Marie-Antoinette
24 October	*Report on the Introduction of the Revolutionary Calendar*

Year II (22 September 1793–21 September 1794)

30 October	Closure of the Society of Revolutionary and Republican Women
31 October	Execution of leading Girondins
7 November	Gobel resigns as archbishop of Paris
10 November	'Festival of Liberty' in Paris
14 November	Chabot denounces 'foreign plot'
4 December	Law on revolutionary government centralises power under the Committee of Public Safety
5 December	Camille Desmoulins launches *Vieux Cordelier*
6 December	Convention asserts principle of freedom of religious worship
17 December	Vincent and Ronsin arrested
25 December	Robespierre's *Report on the Principles of Revolutionary Government*
13 January	Arrest of Fabre d'Eglantine
2 February	Release of Vincent and Ronsin
26 February and 3 March (8 and 13 Ventôse)	Saint-Just introduces 'Ventôse decrees'
13–14 March	Arrest of Hébert, Vincent, Ronsin, and Cordeliers club leaders
24 March	Execution of Hébertistes
27 March	Abolition of Paris revolutionary army
30–31 March	Arrest of Danton, Desmoulins, and leading Indulgents
5 April	Execution of Dantonists
16 April	Committee of Public Safety sets up its own police bureau
7 May	Convention decrees the Cult of the Supreme Being
8 May	Revolutionary tribunals and military commissions outside Paris closed down
11 May	Convention approves Great Book of National Charity
22 May	Assassination attempt on Robespierre and Collot d'Herbois
23 May	Arrest of Cécile Renault
8 June	Festival of the Supreme Being
10 June (22 Prairial)	Law of 22 Prairial simplifies procedures of the revolutionary tribunal
15 June	Vadier reports on the Cathérine Théot affair

26 June	Battle of Fleurus
22–23 July	Attempted reconciliation between the committees of government and Robespierre
23 July	Paris Commune publishes new maximum for Paris
26 July	Robespierre attacks critics in the Convention
27 July	Arrest of Maximilien and Augustin Robespierre, Saint-Just, Couthon and Lebas; all five are dead by the following day
29 July	Convention votes to renew a quarter of the personnel of its committees monthly
1 August	The law of 22 Prairial repealed
10 August	Reorganisation of the revolutionary tribunal
24 August	Powers of the Committee of Public Safety reduced

Year III (22 September 1794–22 September 1795)

12 November	Paris Jacobin club closed down
16 December	Execution of Carrier for *noyades* in Nantes
1 April	Sans-culottes invade the Convention to demand 1793 constitution and food price controls
20 May	Sans-culotte insurrection for 'bread and the 1793 constitution' is defeated
31 May	Abolition of revolutionary tribunal
22 August	Constitution of Year III adopted

Year IV (23 September 1795–21 September 1796)

| 26 October | Last session of the Convention |
| 3 November | Directory takes office |

Bibliography

Unless otherwise stated, the place of publication for all books listed here is London (for works in English) or Paris (for works in French).

General histories

[1] F. Aftalion, *The French Revolution. An Economic Interpretation* (1990). An economic history of the revolution which stresses the role played by poor financial policy and currency inflation in causing the terror; overstates its case.

[2] F.-A. Aulard, *The French Revolution. A Political History, 1789– 1804* (trans. 1910). The classic republican interpretation of the revolution, of the era of the Third Republic, with a clear statement of the 'circumstance' explanation of the terror.

[3] T. C. W. Blanning (ed.), *The Rise and Fall of the French Revolution* (1996). Important collection of articles, some of which are listed below.

[4] W. Doyle, *The Oxford History of the French Revolution* (1989). The best modern text on the revolution: readable and well balanced.

[5] F. Furet & M. Ozouf (eds), *Critical Dictionary of the French Revolution* (trans. Cambridge, Mass., 1989). The Furet view of the revolution in thematic format: stimulating and controversial.

[6] F. Furet & D. Richet, *The French Revolution* (trans. 1970). Furet's first attack on the Marxist approach to the revolution, later superseded by [27] below.

[7] P. Gaxotte, *La Révolution française* (1970). Modern version of the traditional right-wing interpretation of the revolution.

[8] P. Higonnet, *Sister Republics. The Origins of French & American Republicanism* (1989). Interesting revisionist comparison of the

different directions followed by the American and French revolutions.

[9] C. Jones, *The Longman Companion to the French Revolution* (1988). A useful reference book for people, places and dates.

[10] P. Jones (ed.), *The French Revolution in Social and Political Perspective* (1996). Important collection of articles, listed individually below.

[11] Georges Lefebvre, *The French Revolution*, 2 vols (1962). One of the best general histories of the revolution, based on a Marxist-style approach.

[12] S. Schama, *Citizens. A Chronicle of the French Revolution* (1989). Superb revisionist narrative of the ancien régime and revolution packed with anecdote and argument; handle with care.

[13] S. F. Scott & B. Rothaus (eds), *Historical Dictionary of the French Revolution, 1789–1799* (1985). Indispensable reference book.

[14] D. Sutherland, *France 1789–1815. Revolution and Counter-revolution* (1985). A general history of the revolution which stresses the importance of counter-revolution.

[15] J. M. Thompson, *The French Revolution* (1944). Written by the leading British historian of the revolution during the first half of the twentieth century, strongly influenced by Aulard and Mathiez.

[16] A. de Tocqueville, *L'Ancien régime* (Oxford, 1962). Influential nineteenth-century analysis of the revolution used by both revisionist and 'circumstance' historians.

Historiography

[17] K. M. Baker (ed.), *The French Revolution and the Creation of Modern Political Culture. Volume 1. The Political Culture of the Old Regime* (Oxford, 1987). Contains important essays listed below.

[18] K. M. Baker (ed.), *The French Revolution and the Creation of Modern Political Culture. Volume 4. The Terror* (Oxford, 1994). Contains essays listed below.

[19] K. M. Baker, *Inventing the French Revolution* (1992). Collection of articles on the intellectual origins of the revolution.

[20] T. C. W. Blanning, *The French Revolution* (1991, second edition).

Excellent introduction to the debate on the revolution's social origins.

[21] E. Burke, *Reflections on the Revolution in France* (1790, various editions). Not easy to read, but worth consulting for Burke's denunciation of the revolution.

[22] P. Calvert, 'Terror in the Theory of Revolution', in N. O'Sullivan (ed.), *Terrorism, Ideology and Revolution* (Brighton, 1986). An attempt to explore the role of terror in modern revolutions.

[23] J. R. Censer, 'The Coming of a New Interpretation of the French revolution', *Journal of Social History*, 21 (1988). A review of the revisionist arguments which airs doubts over the influence of Rousseau's thought in 1789.

[24] A. Cobban, *The Social Interpretation of the French Revolution* (1964). The first modern challenge to the 'Marxist' interpretation of the revolution; superseded by more recent research.

[25] P. Farmer, *France Reviews Its Revolutionary Origins. Social and Political Opinion in the Third Republic* (1944). Excellent guide to historical writing on the revolution during the Third Republic (1870–1940).

[26] J. Friguglietti, 'Alphonse Aulard: Radical Historian of the Radical Republic', *Proceedings of the Annual Meeting of the Western Society for French History*, 14 (1987). Traces Aulard's early career and approach to the revolution.

[27] F. Furet, *Interpreting the French Revolution* (trans. 1981). The collection of essays which launched the revisionist approach to the revolution and terror.

[28] F. Furet, 'A Commentary', *French Historical Studies*, 16, no. 4 (1990). Furet explains his belief that the fundamental radicalism of the revolution was a product of ideology as early as 1789.

[29] A. Gérard, *La Révolution française, mythes et interprétations* (1970). A useful short survey of the historiography of the revolution.

[30] N. Hampson, 'The French Revolution and Its Historians', in G. Best (ed.), *The Permanent Revolution. The French Revolution and Its Legacy 1789–1799* (1988). Best introduction to revolutionary historiography for beginners.

[31] E. J. Hobsbawm, *Echoes of the Marseillaise. Two Centuries Look Back on the French Revolution* (1990). Wide-ranging historiographical survey from Britain's leading Marxist historian.

[32] L. Hunt, 'Review Essay. Penser la Révolution Française', *History & Theory*, 20 (1981). An early critique of Furet's revisionism.

[33] S. Kaplan, *Adieu 89* (1993). A stunning survey of the bicentenary's historical controversies and historians.

[34] C. Lucas (ed.), *The French Revolution and the Creation of Modern Political Culture. Volume 2. The Political Culture of the French Revolution* (Oxford, 1988). Collection of important essays, several of which are cited elsewhere in this bibliography.

[35] J. McManners, 'The Historiography of the French Revolution', in A. Goodwin (ed.), *New Cambridge Modern History, Volume 8* (Cambridge, 1965). Strong on the nineteenth-century historians of the revolution.

[36] A. Mathiez, *Le Bolchévisme et le Jacobinisme* (Paris, 1920). A naive comparison of Lenin and Robespierre written just after the Bolshevik revolution which asserts that 'history is repeating itself exactly'.

[37] S. Maza, 'Politics, Culture & the Origins of the French Revolution', *Journal of Modern History*, 61 (1989). Also in [10] above. A review essay on [17] above which outlines its innovations but also expresses reservations about the reliance on textual analysis.

[38] S. Mellon, *The Political Use of History. A Study of Historians in the French Restoration* (Stanford, 1958). See chapter 2 for the approach of historians such as Mignet in the 1815–30 period.

[39] L. G. Mitchell (ed.), *The Writings and Speeches of Edmund Burke. Volume VIII. The French Revolution 1790–1794* (Oxford, 1989). A useful introduction which puts Burke's ideas in their context.

[40] B. Nelms, *The Third Republic & the Centennial of 1789* (1987). The political background to the 1889 celebrations.

[41] J. L. Talmon, *The Origins of Totalitarian Democracy* (1952). Argues that the Enlightenment created a messianic approach to politics which stifled liberalism in the French revolution and led to the development of totalitarian regimes in the twentieth century.

[42] M. Vovelle, '1789–1917: The Game of Analogies', in [18] above. A shrewd look at French and Russian historical writing on the revolution between 1917 and 1941.

[43] I. Woloch, 'On the Latent Illiberalism of the French Revolution', *American Historical Review*, 95, no. 5 (1990). Well informed criticism of the revisionist approach.

Early revolution: 1789–1792

[44] H. B. Applewhite, *Political Alignments in the French National Assembly 1789–1791* (1993). Detailed analysis of political groups in the National Assembly: indispensable.

[45] A. de Baecque, 'Quand le cochon symbolisait Louis XVI', *L'Histoire*, 98 (March 1987). Political cartoonists rarely show respect for persons, or for pigs.

[46] K. M. Baker, 'Fixing the French Constitution', in [19] above. An important article on the constitutional debates of 1789.

[47] K. M. Baker, 'Representation redefined', in [17] and [19] and above. Explores the constitutional debates of 1789 and argues that they left the question of popular sovereignty unresolved.

[48] K. M. Baker, 'Revolution', in [34] above. Traces the way in which 1789 changed ideas on the nature of revolution.

[49] T. C. W. Blanning, *The French Revolutionary Wars 1787–1802* (1996). Clear and trenchant analysis of the diplomatic history of the 1790s.

[50] T. C. W. Blanning, *The Origins of the French Revolutionary Wars* (1986). Traces the reasons for the revolution's drift towards war in the spring of 1792: not pleasant reading for Girondins.

[51] J. R. Censer, *Prelude to Power. The Parisian Radical Press 1789–1791* (1976). A good analysis of the early radical press in Paris.

[52] W. Doyle, *The Origins of the French Revolution* (1980). Written too early to include the revisionist argument but excellent on the social and political origins.

[53] D. Echevarria, 'The Pre-revolutionary Influence of Rousseau's *Contrat Social*', *Journal of the History of Ideas*, 33 (1972). Argues that the influence of Rousseau's political ideas were overshadowed by that of his other writings prior to 1789.

[54] F. Furet & R. Halévi, *Orateurs de la Révolution Française. Volume I. Les Constituants* (1989). The introduction argues that the radicalism of the revolution was already present in 1789.

[55] J. Godechot, *The Counter-Revolution: Doctrine & Action 1789–1804* (1972). Useful survey of the counter-revolution.

[56] J. Godechot, *The Taking of the Bastille. July 14th 1789* (trans. 1970). Provides background and detail on the event.

[57] L. Gottschalk & M. Maddox, *Lafayette in the French Revolution, Through the October Days* (Chicago, 1969). A meticulous study of Lafayette's role until late 1789.

[58] H. Gough, *The Newspaper Press in the French Revolution* (1988). A survey of the Parisian and provincial newspaper press.

[59] D. Greer, *The Incidence of the Emigration During the French Revolution* (Cambridge, Mass., 1951). Covers the numerical and geographical impact of emigration.

[60] R. Griffiths, *Le centre perdu. Malouet et les 'monarchiens' dans la révolution française* (Grenoble, 1988). Traces the failure of the monarchiens through the biography of one of their leaders, Pierre-Victoire Malouet.

[61] N. Hampson, *Prelude to Terror. The Constituent Assembly and the Failure of Consensus 1789–1791* (1988). An analysis of the debates of the National Assembly which emphasises the influence of Rousseau.

[62] J. Hardman, *Louis XVI* (1993). Modern biography of an enigmatic king which paints a sympathetic portrait.

[63] L. Hunt, 'The National Assembly', in [17] above. Brings out the significance of the events of June 1789.

[64] P. M. Jones, *The Peasantry in the French Revolution* (1988). Surveys the impact of the revolution on the peasantry.

[65] P. M. Jones, *Reform & Revolution in France. The Politics of Transition 1789–1791* (1995). Chapter 6 provides an excellent account of the reforms of 1789–1791.

[66] M. Kennedy, *The Jacobin Clubs in the French Revolution. The First Years* (1982). Puts the Jacobin clubs in Paris and the provinces under the microscope.

[67] G. Lewis, *The Second Vendée. The Continuity of Counter-Revolution in the Department of the Gard 1789–1815* (1978). Probes the religious and social background to conflict in the Gard.

[68] M. Lewis-Beck, A. Hildreth & A. B. Spitzer, 'Y a-t-il eu un groupe girondin à la Convention Nationale?', in F. Furet & M. Ozouf, *La Gironde et les Girondins* (1991). Broadly endorses the view of the Girondins in [156] below, emphasising their increasing cohesion in the spring of 1793.

[69] C. Lucas, 'The Problem of the Midi in the French Revolution', *Transactions of the Royal Historical Society*, 5th series, 28 (1978). Stimulating article on the factors behind the prevalence of violence in many parts of southern France.

[70] B. Luttrell, *Mirabeau* (1990). A readable and well documented account of his political acrobatics from 1789 to 1791.

[71] J. McManners, *The French Revolution & the Church* (1969). Best

account in English of the revolution's relations with the Catholic Church.

[72] C. J. Mitchell, *The French Legislative Assembly of 1791* (Leiden, 1989). Reviews the politics of the Assembly.

[73] C. J. Mitchell, 'Political Divisions Within the Legislative Assembly of 1791', *French Historical Studies*, 13 (1984). Analyses voting patterns in the Legislative Assembly.

[74] W. Murray, *The Right Wing Press in the French Revolution 1789–1792* (1986). Valuable for the ideology of the right wing press.

[75] M. Ozouf, 'Public Opinion at the end of the Old Régime', *Journal of Modern History*, 60 (1988). Reviews the development of public opinion under the ancien régime, showing its failure to encourage political pluralism.

[76] J. Roberts, *The Counter-Revolution in France 1787–1830* (1990). An excellent brief survey: see especially chapters 1 and 2.

[77] R. B. Rose, *The Making of the Sans-Culottes. Democratic Ideas and Institutions in Paris, 1789–1792* (1983). Traces the growth of early sans-culotte radicalism.

[78] G. Rudé, *The Crowd in the French Revolution* (1959). The motives and activities of the Paris crowd: a modern classic.

[79] P. Sagnac, 'La composition des Etats-Généraux et de l'Assemblée Nationale (1789). Etude statistique et sociale', *Revue Historique*, 206 (1951). Surveys the social and intellectual background of deputies to all three estates.

[80] S. F. Scott, 'Problems of Law & Order During 1790, the "Peaceful" Year of the French Revolution', *American Historical Review*, 80 (1975). Argues that it was far from peaceful and underlines the instability caused by counter-revolution.

[81] S. F. Scott, *The Response of the Royal Army to the French Revolution: The Role and Development of the Line Army, 1787–1793* (Oxford, 1973). Excellent analysis of the impact of the revolution on the army and its role in 1789.

[82] B. M. Shapiro, *Revolutionary Justice in Paris 1789–1790* (Cambridge, 1993). Traces the transition from ancien régime to revolution and argues that attitudes remained remarkably tolerant towards dissent and counter-revolution.

[83] T. Tackett, *Becoming a Revolutionary. The Deputies of the French National Assembly and the Emergence of a Revolutionary Culture (1789–1790)* (1996). The most detailed political history of the

Assembly yet: holes the revisionist interpretation below the water line.

[84] T. Tackett, *Religion, Revolution and Regional Culture in Eighteenth-Century France. The Ecclesiastical Oath of 1791* (1986). Much more than the title suggests: an analysis of regional religious attitudes.

[85] T. Tackett, 'The Constituent Assembly & the Terror', in [18] above. Argues that there is no direct link between the early revolution and the terror.

[86] T. Tackett, 'Nobles & Third Estate in the Revolutionary Dynamic of the National Assembly, 1789–1790', *American Historical Review*, 94 (1989). Also in [10] above. Essential analysis of the political conflicts of the early months of the Constituent Assembly.

Republic and terror: 1792–4

[87] J. Abray, 'Feminism in the French Revolution', *American Historical Review*, 80 (1975), and in [10] above. Traces the growth of revolutionary feminism and feminist leaders.

[88] J. Bernet, 'La déchristianisation dans le district de Compiègne', *Annales Historiques de la Révolution Française*, 248 (1982). Useful regional study.

[89] J.-P. Bertaud, *The Army of the French Revolution. From Citizen Soldiers to Instruments of Power* (trans. 1988). Excellent on the impact of the revolution on the army.

[90] J.-P. Bertaud, *Camille et Lucille Desmoulins. Un couple dans la tourmente* (1985). Written in a romantic style but based on solid research.

[91] R. Bienvenu (ed.), *The Ninth Thermidor. The Fall of Robespierre* (1968). A valuable collection of documents on the collapse of the revolutionary government.

[92] C. Blum, *Rousseau & the Republic of Virtue. The Language of Politics in the French Revolution* (1986). Argues that Rousseau's concept of virtue affected the revolutionary generation.

[93] M. Bouloiseau, *Le comité de salut public* (1968). Schematic but informative.

[94] P. Boutier & P. Boutry, *Atlas de la Révolution Française. Volume 6. Les sociétés politiques* (1992). The latest research on the growth of Jacobin clubs between 1789 and 1794.

[95] N. Bossut, 'Aux origines de la déchristianisation dans la Nièvre: Fouché, Chaumette ou les Jacobins nivernais?', *Annales Historiques de la Révolution française*, 264 (1986). The political factors behind Fouché's de-Christianisation activity in the Nièvre.

[96] J.-J. Brégeon, *Carrier et la terreur nantaise* (1987). A detailed but unsympathetic account of Carrier's life and his activity in Nantes.

[97] J. Brooman, *The Reign of Terror in France. Jean-Baptiste Carrier and the Drownings at Nantes* (1986). A resource pack with useful source material on the *noyades*.

[98] F. Brunel, *Thermidor 1794: la chute de Robespierre* (1989). Fascinating analysis of the politics of the terror from autumn 1793 until Thermidor.

[99] J. M. Burney, 'The Fear of the Executive and the Threat of Conspiracy: Billaud-Varenne's Terrorist Rhetoric in the French Revolution', *French History*, 5 (1991). An interesting explanation of the way in which one of the more radical members of the Committee of Public Safety became obsessed with the need to eradicate plots and conspiracies.

[100] P. Caron, *Les massacres de septembre* (1935). Detailed and balanced account of the September massacres.

[101] R. C. Cobb, *The People's Armies. Instrument of the Terror in the Departments. April 1793 to Floréal Year II* (trans. 1987). The classic study of the revolutionary armies and of sans-culotte mentality.

[102] R. C. Cobb, *The Police and the People. French Popular Protest 1789-1820* (1970). Typically iconoclastic views on sans-culotte radicalism.

[103] R. C. Cobb, 'Quelques aspects de la mentalité révolutionnaire (avril 1793–thermidor an II)', in R. C. Cobb, *Terreur et subsistences 1793–1795* (1965). A pen portrait of the mental world of the sans-culottes.

[104] M. Crook, *Toulon in War and Revolution. From the Ancien Régime to the Restoration, 1750–1820* (1991). Chapter 6 has the definitive study of the federalist revolt in Toulon.

[105] M. Crook, 'Le fédéralisme et le vote sur la constitution de 1793', in Centre Méridional d'Histoire, *Les Fédéralismes. Réalités et représentations 1789–1874* (Aix-en-Provence, 1995). Some details on the voting patterns for the 1793 constitution.

[106] M. Dorigny, 'Violence et révolution: les Girondins et les massacres de septembre', in A. Soboul (ed.), *Actes du colloque*

Girondins et Montagnards (1980). Shows that the Girondins had few problems with the violence of the September massacres until after the event.

[107] D. L. Dowd, *Pageant Master of the French Republic. Jacques-Louis David and the French Revolution* (1948). Puts the artist in his political context.

[108] A.-M. Duport, 'Commission Populaire d'Orange', in A. Soboul (ed.), *Dictionnaire historique de la révolution française* (1989). A short article on the commission which enforced terror in Orange in 1794.

[109] W. Edmonds, 'Federalism & Urban Revolt in France in 1793', *Journal of Modern History*, 1 (1983). Also in [3] above. Shrewd survey of recent writing on the 'federalist' revolt of 1793.

[110] W. Edmonds, 'A Jacobin Debacle: the Losing of Lyon in 1793', *History*, 54 (1984). Shows the incompetence and unpopularity of Jacobins in Lyon.

[111] W. Edmonds, *Jacobinism & the Revolt of Lyon 1789–1793* (Oxford, 1990). First-rate analysis of Jacobinism and terror in the country's second city.

[112] M. Eude, 'Le comité de sûreté générale en 1793–1794', *Annales Historiques de la Révolution Française*, 261 (1985). Reviews the friction within the governing committees during the summer of 1794.

[113] M. Eude, 'La loi de prairial', *Annales Historiques de la Révolution Française*, 254 (1983). Hopefully the last word on the background to the Prairial law.

[114] M. Eude, 'Points de vue sur l'affaire Cathérine Théot', *Annales Historiques de la Révolution Française*, 198 (1969). Examines the role of the Théot affair in widening divisions within the revolutionary government.

[115] F. Feher, *The Frozen Revolution: An Essay on Jacobinism* (1987). Chapter 5 argues the case for seeing the king's execution as the first step in the terror.

[116] A. Forrest, 'Federalism', in [10] and [34] above. An overview from the leading specialist.

[117] A. Forrest, *The French Revolution and the Poor* (1981). Chapter 5 is good on legislation during the terror.

[118] A. Forrest, *Society & Politics in Revolutionary Bordeaux* (1975). Stresses the political moderation behind the city's federalism in 1793.

[119] F. Furet, 'Terror', in [5] above. The Furet version of the terror in distilled form.

[120] L. Gershoy, *Bertrand Barère. A Reluctant Terrorist* (1962). Biography of the one of the revolution's great survivors.

[121] J. L. Godfrey, *Revolutionary Justice: A Study of the Organisation, Personnel and Procedure of the Paris Tribunal 1793–1795* (Chapel Hill, 1951). A study of the development of the institution rather than its victims.

[122] L. Gottschalk, *Jean Paul Marat. A Study in Radicalism* (1967). Brief biography of the polemical 'friend of the people'.

[123] H. Gough, 'Genocide & the Bicentenary: the French Revolution and the Revenge of the Vendée', *Historical Journal*, 30 (1987). A review of the genocide controversy in the Vendée.

[124] D. Greer, *The Incidence of the Terror During the French Revolution* (1935). The classic analysis of the death toll of the terror.

[125] J. Guilhaumou, *1793. La mort de Marat* (1989). Deals with the context and consequences of Marat's murder.

[126] N. Hampson, 'From Regeneration to Terror: The Ideology of the French Revolution', in N. O'Sullivan (ed.), *Terrorism, Ideology & Revolution* (Brighton, 1986). Hampson has long argued for the importance of ideological factors in bringing on the terror, although in a more balanced way than many revisionists.

[127] N. Hampson, *Danton* (1978). Balanced biography of a controversial figure.

[128] N. Hampson, *The Life & Opinions of Maximilien Robespierre* (1974). A fascinating and unorthodox study of a most controversial revolutionary.

[129] N. Hampson, 'François Chabot & His Plot', *Transactions of the Royal Historical Society*, 5th series, 26 (1976). The clearest possible explanation of the murky underworld of the terror.

[130] N. Hampson, *Saint-Just* (1981). Traces a pessimistic view of Saint-Just's evolution from idealism towards terror.

[131] P. Hanson, *Provincial Politics in the French Revolution: Caen and Limoges, 1789–1794* (1989). Chapter 5 contains valuable material on the federalist revolt in Caen.

[132] P. Higonnet, 'The Social & Cultural Antecedents of Revolutionary Discontinuity: Montagnards & Girondins', *English Historical Review*, 100 (1985). Picks over the differences between Girondins and Montagnards, concluding that 'shared principles and tactical difference' lie at the heart of the split.

[133] O. Hufton, *Women and the Limits of Citizenship in the French Revolution* (1992). Chapter 1 provides a perceptive analysis of women's political activity in the revolution, including the Society of Republican and Revolutionary Women.

[134] E. Kennedy, *A Cultural History of the French Revolution* (1989). Useful study of the cultural policies and impact of the revolution.

[135] L. Jacob, *Joseph Le Bon 1765–1795. La terreur à la frontière (Nord et Pas-de-Calais)*, 2 vols (1938). Details of the terror carried out by Le Bon in the summer of 1794.

[136] D. P. Jordan, *The King's Trial. Louis XVI versus the French Revolution* (1979). Clear and readable account of the events surrounding the trial.

[137] G. Lefebvre, 'Sur la loi du 22 prairial', in G. Lefebvre, *Etudes sur la révolution française* (1954). To be read in conjunction with Eude's study of the Prairial law in [114] above.

[138] C. Lucas, *The Structure of the Terror. The Example of Javogues and the Loire* (1973). Case study of the activities of an unruly representative on mission.

[139] C. Lucas, 'Themes in Southern Violence after 9 thermidor', in G. Lewis & C. Lucas (eds), *Beyond the Terror. Essays in French Regional and Social History, 1794–1815* (1983). Valuable essay on the development of the white terror after 1794.

[140] M. Lyons, 'The 9 Thermidor: Motives and Effects', *European Studies Review*, 55 (1975). Also in [10] above. Useful survey of events leading up to the fall of Robespierre.

[141] P. Mansfield, 'Collot d'Herbois & the Dechristianisers', *Journal of Religious History*, 14 (1986–7). Argues that Collot was little involved in de-Christianisation in Lyon, but carries useful details on its development elsewhere.

[142] P. Mansfield, 'Collot d'Herbois at the Committee of Public Safety: A Revaluation', *English Historical Review*, 308 (1988). Argues the case for Collot as a pragmatist rather than an extremist.

[143] P. Mansfield, 'The Management of Terror in Montagnard Lyon, Year II', *European History Quarterly*, 20 (1990). Analysis of Collot's enforcement of terror in Lyon.

[144] P. Mansfield, 'The Repression of Lyon 1793–4: Origins, Responsibility & Significance', *French History*, 2 (1988). The best account of the repression of federalism in Lyon.

[145] J.-Cl. Martin, *La Vendée et la France* (1987). A balanced view of the Vendée revolt.

[146] J. Matharan, 'Les arrestations des suspects en 1793 et l'an II. Professions and répression', *Annales Historiques de la Révolution Française*, 263 (1986). A statistical analysis of over 9000 arrests in Paris during the terror.

[147] A. Mathiez, *Le dix août* (1934). Still the best short account of the removal of the king on 10 August 1792.

[148] A. Mathiez, 'La Terreur, instrument de la politique sociale des robespierristes', in A. Mathiez, *Girondins et Montagnards* (1930). Makes an unconvincing claim that the ventôse decrees were part of an intended social revolution.

[149] C. Mazauric, 'Political Clubs & Sociability in Revolutionary France, 1790–1794', in D. Dickson, D. Keogh & K. Whelan (eds), *The United Irishmen. Republicanism, Radicalism & Rebellion* (1993). The best account of the spread of Jacobin clubs during the terror.

[150] R. Monnier, 'La dissolution des sociétés populaires parisiennes au printemps de l'an II', *Annales Historiques de la Révolution Française*, 268 (1987). Charts the closure of popular societies after Hébert's execution.

[151] M. Ozouf, *La Fête révolutionnaire, 1789–1799* (1978). Traces the changing shape of role of public ceremonies and celebrations during the decade.

[152] M. Ozouf, 'La revolution française et l'idée de l'homme nouveau', in [34] above. Traces the development of ideas of social and moral regeneration from the ancien régime to the revolution.

[153] M. Ozouf, 'War and Terror in French Revolutionary Discourse (1792–1794)', *Journal of Modern History*, 56 (1984). Sets out to disprove the link between war and terror but uses too narrow a range of source material.

[154] R. R. Palmer, *Twelve Who Ruled. The Year of the Terror in the French Revolution* (Princeton, 1941). Dated but still a very readable account of the Committee's work.

[155] R. R. Palmer, *The Improvement of Humanity. Education and the French Revolution* (Princeton, 1985). Chapters 4 and 5 cover the educational reforms of the terror.

[156] A. Patrick, *The Men of the First French Republic. Political Alignments in the National Convention of 1792* (1972). Still the most reliable analysis of Girondin strength and personnel.

[157] C. Petitfrère, 'The Origins of the Civil War in the Vendée', *French History*, 2 (1988). Also in [10] above. A balanced summary of recent research into the origins of the revolt.

[158] C. Petitfrère, 'Le peuple contre la révolution française', *Histoire*, 53 (1988). A brief review of the anti-recruitment riots in the spring of 1793 which suggests why the Vendée alone developed into a civil war.

[159] R. Pillorget, 'The Cultural Programmes of the 1789 Revolution', *History* 70, (1985). A concise account of several of the cultural innovations of the terror.

[160] R. B. Rose, *The Enragés. Socialists of the French Revolution?* (1965). Although they were neither socialists nor a coordinated political party, this study shows the reasons for their brief period of political influence during the summer of 1793.

[161] W. Scott, *Terror & Repression in Revolutionary Marseille* (1973). Excellent on the origins and repression of federalism in Marseille.

[162] S. Sirich, *The Revolutionary Committees in the Departments of France* (1943). Traces the activities of the crucially important revolutionary committees, which had extensive police powers.

[163] M. Slavin, *The Making of an Insurrection. Parisian Sections and the Gironde* (1986). Detailed study of the insurrection of 2 June 1793.

[164] A. Soboul, *The Parisian Sans-Culottes & the French Revolution 1793–4* (trans. 1964). The middle, analytical section of Soboul's monumental study of the sans-culottes [166].

[165] A. Soboul, 'Saintes patriotes et martyres de la liberté', in A. Soboul (ed.), *Paysans, sans-culottes et Jacobins* (1966). Analysis of the cult of revolutionary martyrs which formed around Lepeletier, Chalier and Marat in the autumn of 1793.

[166] A. Soboul, *Les sans-culottes parisiens en l'an II* (1958). Massive detail on sans-culotte political activity during the terror.

[167] M. Sydenham, *The Girondins* (1961). Sydenham's attempt to deny the existence of a Girondin group; largely superseded by Patrick in [156] above.

[168] T. Tackett, 'The West in France in 1789: The Religious Factor in the Origins of Counterrevolution', *Journal of Modern History*, 54 (1982). Also in [3] above. Indispensable for understanding the religious roots of the revolt in the Vendée.

[169] J. M. Thompson, *Robespierre* (1935). Dated but still valuable biography.

[170] C. Tilly, *The Vendée* (Cambridge, Mass., 1964). The first attempt to explain the Vendée revolt in social terms.

[171] M. Vovelle, *The Revolution Against the Church. From Reason to the Supreme Being* (trans., Oxford, 1991). A comprehensive analysis of the impact of de-Christianisation by the leading scholar in the field.

[172] M. Walzer, *Regicide and Revolution* (1974). Reviews the issues raised by the trial of Louis XVI in a comparative perspective.

[173] M. Walzer, 'The King's Trial and the Political Culture of the Revolution', in [34] above. Accepts the king's execution as a form of political justice, but argues that it was justifiable in its context and was not inexorably linked to the terror which followed.

[174] L. Whaley, 'Political factions and the Second Revolution: The Insurrection of 10 August 1792', *French History*, 7 (1993). Argues that not all Girondins opposed the insurrection of 10 August 1792.

Aftermath

[175] B. Baczko, *Ending the Terror. The French Revolution After Robespierre* (Cambridge, 1994). Important essays on attitudes towards the terror after Thermidor.

[176] R. C. Cobb & G. Rudé, 'Le dernier mouvement populaire de la révolution à Paris. Les journées de germinal et prairial an III', *Revue Historique*, 124 (1955). The death throes of the sans-culotte movement.

[177] M. Lyons, *France Under the Directory* (1975). Clear and readable account of the transition from the terror to the Directory.

[178] A. Maillard, C. Mazauric & E. Walter (eds), *Présence de Babeuf. Lumières, révolution, communisme* (1994). A valuable collection of articles presenting the latest scholarship on Babeuf and his influence.

[179] P. Pilbeam, *Republicanism in Nineteenth Century France, 1814–1871* (1995). An outstanding survey of the fate of the republican tradition during the nineteenth century.

[180] R. Rémond, *The Right Wing in France from 1815 to de Gaulle* (Philadelphia, 1966). Classic analysis of right-wing ideas and ideology since Napoleon.

[181] R. B. Rose, *Gracchus Babeuf. First Revolutionary Communist* (Stanford, 1978). Puts Babeuf's adaptation of Jacobin social policy into context.

[182] K. Tønnesson, *La Défaite des sans-culottes. Mouvement populaire et réaction bourgeoise en l'an III* (1959). Detailed account of the decline of sans-culotte power after Thermidor.

Index

Admirat, Henri, 55
Aix-en-Provence, 72
Arras, 45, 57
Artois, Count of, 14–15
Aulard, Alphonse, 5–6, 56, 63

Babeuf, Gracchus, 79
Baker, Keith Michael, 7
Barère, Bertrand, 45, 70, 71
Barruel, abbé, 3
Bastille, 5, 11, 24, 75, 80
Billaud-Varenne, Jacques
    Nicolas, 37, 45, 58, 69, 71,
    82
Bonaparte, Napoleon, 1, 73, 74,
    79
Bordeaux, 35, 39, 41, 57, 76
Bouchotte, Jean-Baptiste, 55
Bouquier law, 61
Brissot, Jacques Pierre, 22, 26
Burke, Edmund, 3–4

Cabarrus, Thérèse, 42
Caen, 34–5, 41
Cambrai, 57
Carnot, Lazare, 36, 45, 67, 69
Carrier, Jean-Baptiste, 39, 71,
    77, 84
Chabot, François, 49, 83
Champ de Mars, 18, 24, 81

Chaunu, Pierre, 4
circumstance argument, 4–6, 9,
    54, 64, 76–7
civil constitution of the clergy,
    12, 15, 17, 18, 19, 22, 29,
    47, 80
Collot d'Herbois, Jean-Marie,
    37, 39–40, 45, 50, 55, 69,
    71, 82, 83
Committee of General Security,
    55, 68, 70, 71
Committee of Public Safety, 2,
    29, 34, 36, 37, 41, 42, 44–6,
    48, 49, 50, 51, 55, 57, 58,
    59, 60, 61, 62, 63, 64, 67,
    69, 71, 72, 78, 82, 84
Conspiracy of Equals, 79
constitution of 1791, 11
constitution of 1793, 34
Corday, Charlotte, 36, 82
Cordeliers club, 17, 46, 52
Couthon, Georges-Auguste, 40,
    45, 68, 70, 71, 84
Cult of the Supreme Being,
    62–4
    see also Supreme Being

Danton, Georges-Jacques, 36,
    50, 52–3, 54, 68, 82, 83
David, Jacques-Louis, 62, 63

101